UNIVERSITY OF NORTH CAROLINA AT CHAPEL HILL

DEPARTMENT OF ROMANCE LANGUAGES

NORTH CAROLINA STUDIES
IN THE ROMANCE LANGUAGES AND LITERATURES

Founder: URB

Distributed by:

UNIVERSITY OF NORTH CAROLINA PRESS

CHAPEL HILL

North Carolina 27514

U.S.A.

NORTH CAROLINA STUDIES IN THE
ROMANCE LANGUAGES AND LITERATURES
Number 211

REALITY AND EXPRESSION IN THE POETRY OF CARLOS PELLICER

REALITY AND EXPRESSION
IN THE
POETRY OF CARLOS PELLICER

BY

GEORGE MELNYKOVICH

CHAPEL HILL

NORTH CAROLINA STUDIES IN THE ROMANCE
LANGUAGES AND LITERATURES
U.N.C. DEPARTMENT OF ROMANCE LANGUAGES
1979

Library of Congress Cataloging in Publication Data

Melnykovich, George.
Reality and expression in the poetry of Carlos Pellicer.

(North Carolina studies in the Romance languages and literatures;
no. 211)
Bibliography: p.
1. Pellicer, Carlos, 1897- —Criticism and interpretation. I. Title.
II. Series.

PQ7297.P3Z77   861   79-14433
ISBN 0-8078-9211-4

I. S. B. N. 0-8078-9211-4

IMPRESO EN ESPAÑA
PRINTED IN SPAIN

DEPÓSITO LEGAL: V. 2.021 - 1979   I. S. B. N. 84-499-2983-0

ARTES GRÁFICAS SOLER, S. A. - JÁVEA, 28 - VALENCIA (8) - 1979

ACKNOWLEDGMENTS

The source of inspiration and direction of this work are the fruits of two seminars on modern poetry dictated at the University of Pittsburgh. One was taught by Dr. Alfredo Roggiano and the other by Octavio Paz. To Dr. Roggiano I owe my introduction to the poetry of Carlos Pellicer and the critical skills one needs to bring to the study of poetry. To Octavio Paz I express my gratitude for the interest he demonstrated in my work and the insights which he provided.

I thank Mr. and Mrs. John Carr and Hiram College for the resources that made possible the publication of this work. But first and foremost it is Caroline whose love and support helped bring these words to light.

TABLE OF CONTENTS

I

INTRODUCTION

Carlos Pellicer has been, and continues to be, considered one of Mexico's most significant and influential poets of the twentieth century. Early in his poetic career critics of the stature of Alfonso Reyes and Pedro Henríquez Ureña, and writers of fame like Gabriela Mistral and Rodolfo Usigli [1] recognized and lauded the talents of this new poet. More recently the notable contemporary poet and critic of Mexico, Octavio Paz, wrote the following about the poetry of Carlos Pellicer:

> La aparición de Carlos Pellicer... fue deslumbrante. El primer libro de Pellicer (1921) refleja su asombro ante la realidad del mundo. Ese asombro no cesa: en 1966 la realidad lo entusiasma todavía. A nosotros también nos entusiasma esa poesía que hace volar al mundo y convierte en nube a la roca, al bosque en lluvia, al charco en constelación.... Nunca nos cansará esta realidad con alas. Cada vez que leo a Pellicer, *veo* de verdad. [2]

Paz emphasizes the enthusiasm and exhilaration of Pellicer's poetry: his is a poetry dedicated to the beauty and joy of life. His poetic career has spanned more than fifty years, but his youthful optimism has remained a constant.

Although there have been a number of excellent studies dealing with the poetry of Pellicer, we must admit that these are an excep-

---

[1] See bibliography.
[2] Octavio Paz, ed. *Poesía en movimiento* (Mexico: Siglo XXI, 1966), p. 14.

tion rather than a rule. The general poverty, in quality rather than quantity, of the literary criticism of Pellicer's poetry is remarkable given the significant role he has played in the development of literature in modern Mexico.

In an article written by Gabriela Mistral in 1927, Pellicer had the honor (or misfortune) of being dubbed, "Carlos de América". [3] He has never recovered from the weight of that title. This tag seemed to draw the boundaries for much of the literary criticism dealing with his works which was to follow. The great majority of the critical studies listed in our bibliography are concerned either with a discussion of his "Americanismo," or refer to him as a poet of the "paisaje," the tropics in particular. This rather insufficient and narrow view of his poetry obscured and diminished the importance, profundity and complexity of his work. We do not deny the importance of these studies in terms of their contribution to the understanding of the body of Pellicer's poetry, but we do raise objection with the implicit contention of such an approach.

Any study of poetry which dedicates itself exclusively to thematic expression suggests that content is in some way distinct from form. We do not admit such a separation. On the contrary, we maintain that in poetry form and content, theme and style, reality and its expression are indissolubly connected. Furthermore, if we sustain that Pellicer was an important poet in his own time and a significant influence to succeeding generations, we must admit that his importance is based not only on what he says in his poetry, but on how he says it. This study, "Reality and Expression in the Poetry of Carlos Pellicer," adheres to the above contentions. We will deal with the themes of his poetry insofar as they reveal his poetic vision of reality, and his style as the expression of this reality as well as a formulation of an aesthetic.

---

[3] Gabriela Mistral, "Un poeta nuevo de América; Carlos Pellicer Cámara," Repertorio Americano, XIV: 34 (San José, C. R., 1927), p. 373.

II

PELLICER'S AESTHETIC INHERITANCE

As we stated in our introduction, this chapter has two purposes: one, to situate Carlos Pellicer in the appropriate historical perspective; and two, to consider those trends, poets, and works which had a pronounced influence in the aesthetic development of our poet. Thus we do not pretend to make any definitive statements about those trends and writers, but limit ourselves to discussing those characteristics which Pellicer, directly or indirectly, adopted.

A. MODERNISM

Modernism was not solely a literary school, but rather an attitude, a new vision, which received its initial impulse from writers but would permeate all aspects of life and thought.

Modernism was not an isolated movement born in Latin America, but rather the Hispanic form of the revolt against preestablished cultural forms which characterized the development of the arts in the nineteenth century.

We will not enumerate here the technical innovations brought to Hispanic poetry by the Modernist movement since these are well documented in many reputable studies of Latin American literature. The renovation and innovation of versification should not, however, be underestimated in their importance to the poet of the twentieth century. Due in large part to Modernist accomplishments, the modern poet was free to adopt all verse forms, new and ancient, Spanish and foreign, and eventually use any form that was appropriate to his expression.

Central to understanding Modernism's influence on the aesthetic development of Pellicer are the following attitudes or trends: a cosmopolitan spirit; a renewed interest and pride in literary-Americanism; a critical attitude in terms of a world vision, as well as a criticism directed at poetry itself; and a reevaluation of Greco-Roman civilization. [1] Let us briefly examine some of these trends.

Modernism in its initial stages was influenced in great part by Romanticism, the Parnassus and Symbolism. The early Modernists express the Romantic disdain for society, but their solution is not to struggle with this reality, but rather to escape to their ivory tower, symbol of the poet isolated in a world of artificial culture.

From the French poets of the Parnassus the Modernist poet acquired his love for beauty and formal perfection as well as a renewed contact with the Classical Age. The Modernist's quest for technical perfection, "pursuit of form" says Darío, [2] made him conscious of the lyrical effusions, worn-out imagery, poetic clichés, and restrictive metrical forms of Romantic poetry. His reaction to the excesses of Romanticism led to renovation and innovation of metrical forms in search of a form and expression that would reflect the new and modern aesthetic. Form was not seen as a means to an end, but rather an end in itself.

Symbolism's influence on Modernist poets was not exclusively in the area of poetic form. Symbolism intensified the poet's estrangement with nature and gave new meaning to the poetic word. Due in large part to the achievements of the French symbolists, the Modernist began to return to poetic language its lost vitality and freshness.

In his study entitled *From Baudelaire to Surrealism*, Marcel Raymond speaks of the development of poetic language in the modern era in terms of a departure from the "immediate" word, a

---

[1] This Modernist attitude had a most pronounced influence on the "Ateneo de la Juventud" of Mexico, a group of writers and thinkers whose influence on Pellicer we discuss later in this chapter.

[2] Our discussion of Modernism will center on the achievements of Rubén Darío since he is the principal figure of this movement and because of the admitted admiration Pellicer expressed for Darío in an interview: "En Rubén Darío de *Cantos de vida y esperanza* será siempre el testimonio de un altísimo poeta. Y ese libro es fundamentalmente un libro de belleza y está escrito por un poeta genial que fue Darío. Darío es para mí un maestro para siempre." See Appendix for the complete interview.

term for language which is used essentially for "transmission of concepts and ideas," toward the symbolist's attempt at arriving at the "essential" word. As he explains:

> This linguistic art is an experimental and intuitive science of the poetic value and meaning of words, of their reciprocal relations and reactions, a method of reviving the original images and mythical residues that subsist in them. [3]

One can see in the mature Darío a movement towards the "essential" word. His poetry avoids the demonstrative word in favor of a language that is emotive and evocative. His images are not mere embellishment, but attempt to uncover the "correspondences" between words. The movement toward the "essential" word in poetry is evidenced in the latter stages of modernism especially as it entered the twentieth century.

In 1905 Darío publishes *Cantos de vida y esperanza* in which he states in the initial poem:

> Yo soy aquel que ayer no más decía
> el verso azul y la canción profana,
> en cuya noche un ruiseñor había
> que era alondra de luz por la mañana.
> ... ...
> Y la vida es misterio; la luz ciega
> y la verdad inaccesible asombra;
> la adusta perfección jamás se entrega,
> y el secreto ideal duerme en la sombra. [4]

Darío is no longer content to remain in his ivory tower in aristocratic exile. His poetry takes on a more human tone, abandoning the artificiality of some of his previous verse. Form is no longer the sole objective, but a means to understanding the expressing of the human condition. In "Lo fatal" he writes:

> Dichoso el árbol que es apenas sensitivo,
> y más la piedra dura, porque ésta ya no siente,

---

[3] Marcel Raymond, *From Baudelaire to Surrealism* (London: Metheun and Co., 1970), p. 19.
[4] Darío, p. 627.

> pues no hay dolor más grande que el dolor de ser vivo,
> ni mayor pesadumbre que la vida consciente [5]

He is aware of his condition as a human and particularly as a
Latin American. A new sense of pride voiced by writers such as
José Enrique Rodo in *Ariel* (1900) is echoed by Darío in "Saluta-
ción al optimista" and "A Roosevelt." He defends his entry into
poetry of political commitment in his prologue to *Cantos*:

> Si en estos cantos hay política, es porque aparece universal.
> Y si encontráis versos a un presidente, es porque son un
> clamor continental. Mañana podremos ser yanquis (y es
> lo más probable); . . . . [6]

In an article entitled "Rubén Darío y la modernidad" Saúl Yurkievich affirms that modernity for Latin American poetry begins
with Rubén Darío. He gives as the starting point for this modernity
the year 1905 with the publication of *Cantos de vida y esperanza*. [7]
Yurkievich considers Darío the initiator of the avant-garde movement in Latin America saying:

> Darío es el primero en salir del estrecho recinto de las
> literaturas nacionales, el primero en vivir por doquier, en
> abandonar su Nicaragua natal, para instalarse en Chile,
> en la Argentina, después en España, en Francia, en Esta-
> dos Unidos; el primero en preconizar y encabezar un
> movimiento literario internacional, en abrirse con máxima
> receptividad a todos los estímulos, en absorber y propagar
> una amplia, diversa gama de influencias extranjeras, el
> primero en sentirse mundial, actual, en practicar un autén-
> tico cosmopolitismo; también el primero en abolir censu-
> ras morales, en promover una reflexión teórica sobre la

---

[5] Darío, p. 688.

[6] Darío, p. 626. Enrique González Martínez becomes the collective voice
of the post-modernist poets when he publishes the sonnet, "Tuércele el
cuello al cisne" (1910). He calls for the death of the swan, symbol of
disinterested and useless beauty, and brings forth the owl, symbol of
wisdom and introspection, as the representative of the new poetry. It should
be emphasized that the new aesthetic credo voiced by González Martínez
is a synthesis of similar departures from Modernism voiced by several poets
among them, Rubén Darío. See Max Henríquez Ureña. *Breve historia del
modernismo*, p. 496.

[7] Saúl Yurkievich, "Rubén Darío y la modernidad," *Plural*, No. 9 (June,
1972), pp. 37-41.

literatura, en asumir las crisis, las rupturas, el desgarramiento que caracterizan a la conciencia de nuestro tiempo. [8]

While we agree in full with Yurkievich's contentions, any study of Latin American poetry would be incomplete without giving due credit to perhaps the most important individual effort in its development, Leopoldo Lugones.

Leopoldo Lugones established himself as the leader of Argentine modernism with the publication of *Las montañas del oró* (1897) and *Los crepúsculos del jardín* (1905). The poems contained in those works reflect the plasticity, sensorial and pictorial qualities of parnassian verse, as well as the imprecision, the musicality, and the suggestiveness of symbolist poetry.

In *Lunario sentimental* (1909), his poetry reflects a movement away from modernism. This book which has been called the "Manual de la metáfora para toda la generación postmodernista y trampolín de la poesía de vanguardia" [9] is a sally into free verse, monorhyme, prosaic poetry, and the negation of mimesis as the principle for artistic creation. In the prologue to this book he writes:

> el lenguaje es un conjunto de imágenes, comportando, si bien se mira, una metáfora cada vocablo; de manera que hallar imágenes nuevas y hermosas, expresándolas con claridad y concisión, es enriquecer el idioma, renovándolo a la vez. Los encargados de esta obra, tan honorable, por lo menos, como la de refinar los ganados o administrar la renta pública, puesto que se trata de una función social, son los poetas. El idioma es un bien social, y hasta el elemento más sólido de las nacionalidades. [10]

Jorge Luis Borges, once the Argentine ultraist poet, recognizes the achievements of Lugones when he says:

> Yo creo que esa revolución, el ultraísmo, realmente no tenía mucho sentido cuando se hizo, porque ya lo que

---

[8] Yurkievich, "Rubén Darío," p. 37.

[9] Jaime Alazraki, *Poética y poesía de Pablo Neruda* (New York: Las Américas, 1965), p. 26.

[10] Leopoldo Lugones, *Lunario sentimental,* 3rd ed. (Buenos Aires: Ediciones Centurión, 1961), p. 7.

> nosotros nos proponíamos lo había hecho Lugones. Y lo
> ha hecho mejor que nosotros. [11]

Later he adds:

> Además, el programa de Lugones,... ya lo formuló en el
> *Lunario sentimental* de 1909; que no era sólamente la
> renovación de la metáfora, lo que nosotros decíamos, sino
> renovación de métrica; [12]

Alfredo Roggiano agrees with Borges in his estimation of Lugones
when he writes:

> La crítica parece estar de acuerdo en que el *Lunario sen-*
> *timental* (1909) de Leopoldo Lugones es la obra más revo-
> lucionaria y más original de la literatura en lengua espa-
> ñola que siguió inmediatamente al modernismo de *Prosas*
> *profanas.* [13]

Leopoldo Lugones is not only a key figure in the avant-garde
of Argentina and Latin America, especially Mexico where he was
read widely and even imitated, [14] but he also brings forth funda-
mental elements which are related to modernity as criticism of the
modern epoch. Lugones' work had particular significance for the
development of poetry in the generation preceding Pellicer's.
The Argentine poet would find in Ramón López Velarde an ad-
vocate of his metaphorical and metric innovations.

Where González Martínez symbolically [15] announces the culmi-
nation of Modernism and a return to "el alma de las cosas," Ramón
López Velarde embarks on a journey to discover the true essence

---

[11] Cited in Cleon Wade Capsas, *The Poetry of Jorge Luis Borges,* Ph.D.
Dissertation, University of New Mexico, 1964, p. A2.

[12] Capsas, p. A2.

[13] Alfredo Roggiano, "Situación y tendencias de la nueva poesía argentina," Reprint of *The Interamerican Review of Bibliography,* XIII, No. 1,
p. 8.

[14] Pellicer, in an interview with this writer, mentioned Lugones as one
of the poets who influenced his development.

[15] Octavio Paz, *Las peras del olmo,* 2nd ed. (Mexico: Universidad Nacional de México, 1965), p. 82. Paz states: "González Martínez no rompe
con el lenguaje modernista; atenúa sus excesos, vela sus luces, pero se sirve
de las mismas palabras para advertirnos de su falsedad."

of Mexican reality, and in the process, himself. As he writes in "Suave Patria":

> Suave Patria: te amo no cual mito,
> sino por tu verdad de pan bendito,
> como a niña que se asoma por la reja... [16]

The originality and importance of López Velarde to the development of modern poetry is that he is the creator of a new poetic language which has its antecedents in the poetry of Laforgue and Lugones. As Octavio Paz points out:

> En ellos aprende López Velarde el secreto de esas imágenes que mezclan, en dosis explosivas, lo cotidiano con lo inusitado y que un adjetivo incandescente ilumina, arte que participa de la fórmula química y de la magia. [17]

Of the similarities found in the poetry of Laforgue, Lugones and López Velarde, Paz lists: "la rima inesperada, la imagen autosuficiente, la ironía, el dinamismo de los contrastes, el choque entre lenguaje literario y lenguaje hablado." [18]

López Velarde does not fall to mere imitation of his masters but lends an original stroke to the development of a new poetic language. Paz contends that:

> La originalidad de López Velarde consiste en seguir un procedimiento inverso al de sus maestros: no parte del lenguaje poético hacia la realidad, en un viaje descendente que en ocasiones es una caída en lo prosaico, sino que asciende del lenguaje cotidiano hacia uno nuevo, difícil y personal. [19]

B. MODERNISM TO AVANT-GARDE IN MEXICO

The year 1910 has special significance for Mexico. This date marks Mexico's entry, politically, as well as artistically, into the

---

[16] Ramón López Velarde, *Obras*, ed. José Luis Martínez (Mexico: Fondo de Cultura, 1971), p. 38.

[17] Paz, *Las peras del olmo*, p. 95.

[18] Paz, *Las peras del olmo*, p. 95.

[19] Paz, *Las peras del olmo*, p. 95.

modern era. There are two main directions which are related: the first, political, is the Revolution of 1910, a popular based revolt against the tyrannical reign of Porfirio Díaz; the second, cultural, is a movement against Positivism, the official philosophy of the Díaz era. This cultural movement was spearheaded by a group called the "Ateneo de México."

The "Ateneo," whose membership included Alfonso Reyes, González Martínez, José Vasconcelos, Antonio Caso, and Diego Rivera, was strongly influenced by the Dominican, Pedro Henríquez Ureña, who writes of the new intellectual awakening in Mexico:

> El nuevo despertar intelectual de México, como de toda la América Latina en nuestros días, está creando en el país la confianza en su propia fuerza espiritual. México se ha decidido a adoptar la actitud de crítica, de discusión, de prudente discernimiento, y no ya de aceptación respetuosa, ante la producción intelectual y artística de los países extranjeros; espera, a la vez, encontrar en las creaciones de sus hijos las cualidades distintivas que deben ser la base de una cultura original. [20]

The "Ateneo" called for a total reevaluation of the spiritual and intellectual life of Mexico. They established the Popular University of Mexico, introduced the works of modern European writers and philosophers and reemphasized the need to study the classics. [21] The latter is important to the aesthetic development of Pellicer for it demonstrates the need for what Reyes called "tradiciones formativas" [22] in an alternate vision of reality to that of the modern era.

---

[20] Pedro Henríquez Ureña, *Plenitud de América* (Buenos Aires: Peña, del Guidice-Editores, 1952), p. 79.

[21] Pedro Henríquez Ureña writes: "Entonces nos lanzamos a leer a todos los filósofos a quienes el positivismo condenaba como inútiles, desde Platón, que fue nuestro mayor maestro, hasta Kant y Schopenhauer. Tomamos en serio (¡oh blasfemia!) a Nietzsche. Descubrimos a Bergson, a Boutroux, a James, a Croce. Y en la literatura no nos confinamos dentro de la Francia moderna. Leíamos a los griegos, que fueron nuestra pasión." Pedro Henríquez Ureña, *Plenitud...*, p. 80.

[22] Reyes writes: "Se quería volver un poco a las lenguas clásicas y un mucho al castellano; se buscaban las tradiciones formativas, constructivas

The chaotic progression of the Mexican revolution led to the disbanding of the "Ateneo," and, for a short period, literary production was independent of any group or movement. Principal among the poets of this period were the aforementioned González Martínez, López Velarde and José Juan Tablada.

Tablada, who was overshadowed by González Martínez in his time, has, until recent criticism, been relegated to a minor role in the development of modern poetry in Mexico.[23] Such criticism is unjust, and rather surprising in light of the comments of Villaurrutia in an article on the young poets of Mexico:

> Si Enrique González Martínez era, hacia 1918, el dios mayor y casi único de nuestra poesía; si de él partían las inspiraciones, si los jóvenes cantaban con pulmones propios el dolor particular de González Martínez, en oraciones semejantes al tedioso orfeón que en torno de Dios deban entonar los ángeles; necesitamos nuevamente de Adán y de Eva que vinieran a darnos con su rebelión, con su pecado, una tierra nuestra de más amplios panoramas, de mayores libertades; una tierra que ver con nuestros propios ojos. La fórmula será: Adán y Eva = Ramón López Velarde y José Juan Tablada.[24]

Tablada began his literary career as a modernist writing in the *Revista Azul*, a modernist magazine founded by Gutiérrez Nájera, and the *Revista Moderna*. A true cosmopolitan spirit, Tablada left Mexico and traveled to the Orient, Paris and New York City.

As a result of his travels and his exposure to the late advances in poetry, he published three titles which had significance to the succeeding generation of poets, the "Contemporáneos" in particular. In 1919 he published *Un día*, a book of synthetic poems. The following year in New York he added *Li-Po y otros poemas* based on experiments in typography begun by Apollinaire. The third book,

---

de nuestra civilización y de nuestro ser nacional." Alfonso Reyes, "De poesía hispanoamericana," *Pasado inmediato y otros ensayos* (Mexico: El Colegio de México, 1941), p. 55.

[23] Raúl Leiva's excellent study of modern Mexican poetry, *Imagen de la poesía mexicana contemporánea*, omits a study of Tablada.

[24] Xavier Villaurrutia, "La Poesía de los jóvenes de México," *Obras*, 2nd ed. (Mexico: Fondo de Cultura Económica, 1966), p. 825.

also published in New York, was *El jarro de flores*, (1922). These books not only included some of the latest experiments in poetry but more importantly introduced the "haiku" to Hispanic literature.

Although much has been written of the contribution of González Martínez and López Velarde to the development of poetry in twentieth century Mexico, it is, in our estimation, Tablada who makes the most significant inroads to the poetry of modernity. His interest in the Orient, as evidenced by his use of the haiku, is an indirect criticism of modern Western reality. Tablada's poetry is a thrust into the development of the free and self-sufficient image which would represent the nucleus of modern poetry. The haiku can be simply defined as a written painting. In three lines the artist presents a complete, self-sufficient picture as in this haiku of Chine-Jo:

> How readily the firefly glows!
> As readily
> Its light goes out.

And Tablada's image of a watermelon:

> Del verano, roja y fría
> carcajada,
> rebanada
> de sandía.

Or a nocturnal butterfly:

> Devuelve a la desnuda rama,
> nocturna mariposa,
> las hojas secas de tus alas. [25]

Villaurrutia, as we stated earlier, was one of the first critics to realize the importance of Tablada when he wrote, "...José Juan Tablada —que señala en nuestra lírica el viento cambiante de las conquistas nuevas—." [26] And, finally, with an irony learned from Lugones, his poetry becomes both a criticism of his epoch and of the poetic word itself.

---

[25] *Poesía en movimiento*, ed. Octavio Paz (Mexico: Siglo XXI, 1966), p. 446.
[26] Villaurrutia, pp. 826-827.

By 1920 Mexico had returned to relative political calm and the news of the latest artistic developments in Europe found an eager and receptive group of young writers. Schneider observes that there were several magazines and papers in Mexico, *Revista de Revistas, Zig-Zag,* and *El Universal Ilustrado,* that were publishing articles of the avant-garde movements in poetry and painting. Creacionism of Vicente Huidobro received early publicity in Mexico when *Revista de Revistas* published an article on this movement in 1919. The following year *El Universal Ilustrado* published an article entitled "La escuela literaria del día. El creacionismo de Huidobro." [27]

Rafael Lozano, a correspondent for *El Universal Ilustrado,* traveled to Europe and became acquainted with Marinetti, Huidobro, Reverdy, Tristan Tzara, Apollinaire, and other members of the avant-garde movement. Among his articles were studies on futurism, cubism and Dada. [28]

A new "Ateneo" was formed in 1919 by a group of poets who would later form their own respective groups, the most important of which would be "Contemporáneos." Prior to an examination of their work, let us look at a spirited, if short-lived, revolutionary group called the "estridentistas."

1. *Estridentismo*

"Estridentismo," considered to be the first organized avant-garde movement in Mexico, [29] was born with the publication of a flyer called *Actual.* The "estridentista" movement shows the influence of several European "isms' — dadaism, and cubism by the painters of the group — but its ideological and aesthetic inspiration came from futurism, founded by the Italian poet, Felipe Marinetti. *Actual* contains a section in which Maples Arce publishes his fourteen points containing the new aesthetic. Futurism's presence in this aesthetic is made evident in point three which begins with Marinetti's argument that "une automobile rugissante, qui à

[27] Luis Mario Schneider, *El estridentismo* (Mexico: Ediciones de Bellas Artes, 1970), pp. 25-26.
[28] Schneider, pp. 22-23.
[29] Schneider, p. 19.

l'air de courir sur de la mitraille, est plus belle que la Victoire de Samothrace." [30]

The estridentista's infatuation with technology and modern urban society is clearly emphasized in the titles of the books published by the members of the group: *Avión,* by Luis Quintanilla; *Urbe,* Manuel Maples Arce; *El pentagrama-eléctrico* by Salvador Gallardo, etc.

An infatuation with the present and a disdain for the past, the distinguishing characteristics of "estridentismo," would prove to be the eventual pitfalls of its art. The "estridentistas" professed and created an art that was temporal, an art that was old the day after it was created. Thus after the novelty disappeared there was little of substance and value remaining.

The formation of the "estridentista" movement was directly related to the political situation of Mexico during that period. The lengthy revolution had ended its violent phase and a period of reconstruction and stability had begun. Thus the "estridentistas" viewed themselves as revolutionaries. Their mission was to carry the spirit of the Mexican revolution to the field of art. Their rhetoric was revolutionary and their tactics were designed to shock the bourgeoise public and unseat the literary dictators of that period. Feeling the revolution was incomplete and betrayed, the main emphasis of the "estridentista" movement went away from literary revolution to political activism. Unfortunately this redirection had a negative influence on the literary production which deteriorated to political jargon and propaganda.

Although we agree with critics such as Schneider [31] and Leal that "estridentismo" introduced and propagated the new avant-garde trends in literature, this poetry, with few exceptions, never exceeded the stage of novelty and literary shock tactics. The task of making significant and lasting contributions to modern poetry in Mexico was to be accomplished by a group of poets called "Contemporáneos."

---

[30] Schneider, pp. 36-37.
[31] For a complete study of "Estridentismo" see Luis Mario Schneider, *El estridentismo,* cited above.

2. *Contemporáneos*

The name "contemporáneos" refers to a group of poets who collaborated in a literary journal, *Contemporáneos,* published from June, 1928, to December of 1931. But, as it has been pointed out by critics such as Frank Dauster and Merlin Forster, the nucleus of the group was formed prior to 1920. Bernardo Ortiz de Montellano, Jaime Torres Bodet, Enrique González Rojo, José Gorostiza and Carlos Pellicer, all members of the group, were companions in preparatory school and later in the University.

The "Contemporáneos," called by Dauster the most important group in Mexico since Modernism, began publication of the magazine which gave them their name in June of 1928. The editors of the initial effort and the succeeding seven issues were González Rojo, Ortiz de Montellano, and Torres Bodet, who explains the birth of *Contemporáneos:*

> ...Acostumbrados a admitir el prestigio internacional de publicaciones como *Le Mer* y la *N.R.F.*, el éxito de una revista española, *Occidente,* nos había hecho reflexionar sobre la conveniencia de imprimir en nuestro país un órgano literario estricto y bien presentado. Estimábamos las calidades de algunas revistas latinoamericanas, en las cuales a veces colaborábamos. Sin embargo, el eclecticismo de *Nosotros* de Buenos Aires, nos parecía demasiado complaciente. *Ateneo* de Chile adolecía —a nuestro juicio— de un tono un tanto dogmático. Quedaban, en la Habana, la tribuna del grupo *Avance,* en Costa Rica, el heroico *Repertorio* de García Monge. Pero, ¿no había acaso lugar, en México, para una revista distinta, que procurase establecer un contacto entre las realizaciones europeas y las promesas americanas?
>
> Así nació *Contemporáneos,* gracias a la intrepidez del doctor Gastelum y la voluntad de unos cuantos jóvenes, que no se daban cuenta muy clara de las robustas antipatías que su intolerancia imprudente tendría por fuerza que suscitar. [32]

---

[32] Jaimes Torres Bodet, *Tiempo de arena* (Mexico: Fondo de Cultura Económica, 1955), pp. 252-253.

Although there were articles dealing with universal writers and themes, there was a preponderance of Mexican contributors and emphasis on Mexican writers and painters, and a notable absence of socio-political themes. In 1930 Torres Bodet and González Rojo were out of the country on diplomatic missions, and the direction of *Contemporáneos* in August of 1930 went to Ortiz de Montellano. From this point *Contemporáneos* began to broaden its scope from a medium for members of the group to include writers of Spain, Latin America and translations of notable European and North American writers.

Ermilo Abreu Gómez contends that it was Ortiz de Montellano who, in this period of *Contemporáneos,* strongly opposed inclusion of articles dealing with Mexican themes. Those that found their way into the offices of *Contemporáneos* arrived "a escondidas." [33] Thus the magazine, due to Ortiz de Montellano's direction, made a marked turn toward cosmopolitanism and opened the door to avant-garde advancements in art and literature. An examination of *Contemporáneos* during Ortiz de Montellano's tenure will illustrate his emphasis on non-Mexican themes. In July and August of 1930 articles on the poetry of T. S. Eliot and Paul Valery are published. León Felipe, a Spaniard, authors an article on contemporary Spanish poets. In September of 1930 an article on North American poetry appears, while in the April issue of 1931 the surrealist poets, Pablo Neruda and Supervielle are studied. In May of the same year we see a study of the Danish theater by Bontempelli and an article entitled "Principios de forma fílmica" by S. M. Eisenstein. Thus Boyd Carter's assertion that:

> El énfasis en los *Contemporáneos,* conforme al intento de su título, se pone más en valores de índole moderna, nueva, experimental, aún vanguardista, que en el examen y enfoque de los valores culturales ya aceptados y establecidos. Los redactores manifiestan suma predilección por las letras francesas y la literatura "d'avant garde." [34]

---

[33] Ermilo Abreu Gómez, "Contemporáneos," *Las revistas literarias de vanguardia* (Mexico: Instituto Internacional de Literatura Iberoamericana, 1965), p. 77.
[34] Boyd G. Carter, *Las revistas literarias de Hispanoamérica* (Mexico: Ediciones de Andrea, 1959), p. 99.

most accurately pertains to the period of *Contemporáneos* under Ortiz de Montellano's direction.

To list all the achievements of the "contemporáneos" would require an individual study of each of the members of the group. As a group they were responsible for introducing the new tendencies in literature and art, and more important yet, they were responsible for removing Mexico from cultural stagnation due to extreme nationalism which followed the Revolution. Although their interest in non-Mexican themes was a target of much discussion during their formative years, criticism today recognizes the magnitude of their mission and the influence they have demonstrated on all succeeding generations of artists in Mexico.

Pellicer's membership in the group "Contemporáneos" has been a much discussed topic. [35] At first glance he appears unique and, in some cases, antagonistic to the other members. Where the rest of the group was native to the Capital, he was from tropical Tabasco. His poetry is optimistic, joyful and open, while his fellow members border on solitude, pessimism and introspection. His collaboration in the magazine *Contemporáneos* was minimal since during this period he spent much time traveling around the world. He could never, as were his fellow members, be criticized for negating Mexican reality, for that feature is a constant in his work. Pellicer himself points out his peculiarity in the group:

> ...la amistad con los "Contemporáneos" para mí fue fundamentalmente con Novo y Villaurrutia. Novo, en esa época, y durante bastantes años, seguía muy de cerca a la joven poesía norteamericana que influyó mucho en él. Villaurrutia prefería la lectura francesa. Y yo no tenía nada que ver con esas cosas. Yo estaba siempre pensando en la América Latina, en Bolívar, en México, en las culturas prehispánicas. [36]

Thus, using these differences one would feel that Forster was justified in excluding Pellicer from the "Contemporáneos." We, however, feel that Pellicer not only belongs to this group, but is one of the most representative members. Even though the lack of his

---

[35] See studies by Carter, Dauster, Forster and Leiva, cited in the bibliography.

[36] Unpublished interview with the author.

contribution to the group during the publication of the magazine would seem to argue for his exclusion, we feel the link comes with his participation and kinsmanship in the group's formative years and the goals he shared with its members. Forster himself recognizes that one of the goals that the "Contemporáneos" were attempting to achieve was "novedad y universalidad dentro de la cultura mexicana." [37] Pellicer, in his poetry, as we will attempt to demonstrate throughout this study, reaches this end. The evolution of his poetry reflects the influences, direct or indirect, of the latest trends and developments of Spanish American and European avant-garde movements. His assimilation of these new trends is, however, subtle and natural. He is at once very cosmopolitan and yet provincially Mexican.

---

[37] Merlin H. Forster, *Los contemporáneos* (Mexico: Ediciones de Andrea, 1964), p. 14.

III

PELLICER AND CREACIONISM

A. Creacionism

The first two decades of the XXth century shaped the artistic avant-garde in Europe and the Americas and gave birth to a multitude of *isms*. Cubism, Dadaism, Expressionism, Imagism, Futurism, Surrealism, and Ultraism are some of the major movements that formulated modern aesthetic theories. In Latin America the most influential *ism* during the burgeoning years of the avant-garde was Creacionism.

Creacionism, whose chief exponent was the Chilean poet Vicente Huidobro, is clearly an avant-garde movement in the full sense of the word. In *The Theory of the Avant-Garde* Renato Poggioli characterizes the avant-garde as an "activist movement" which is "formed in part or in whole to agitate *against* something or someone." [1] Later he elaborates this idea of activism saying:

> The taste for action for action's sake, the dynamism inherent in the very idea of movement, can in fact drive itself beyond the point of control by any convention or reservation, scruple or limit. It finds joy not merely in the inebriation of movement, but even more in the act of beating down barriers, razing obstacles, destroying whatever stands in its way. [2]

---

[1] Renato Poggioli, *The Theory of the Avant-Garde* (Cambridge, Massachusetts: Harvard University Press, 1968), p. 25.

[2] Poggioli, p. 26.

In addition he mentions avant-garde art as containing a spirit of futurism in the broad sense of the word and not in the confines of the meaning given to it by Marinetti. He contrasts this futurist consciousness of the modern avant-garde period with the consciousness of a classical epoch in which:

> ...it is not the present that brings the past to a culmination, but the past that culminates in the present, and the present is in its turn understood as a new triumph of ancient and eternal values, as a return to the principles of the true and the just, as a restoration or rebirth of those principles. But for the moderns, the present is valid only by virtue of the potentialities of the future, as the matrix of the future, insofar as it is the forge of history in continual metamorphosis, seen as a permanent spiritual revolution. [3]

These attitudes are expressed on numerous occasions in Huidobro's manifestos and his poetry. His program is in direct opposition, or antagonism, to what preceeded him and clearly outlines a plan for the future.

While there have been some disagreements involving Huidobro's originality, recent criticism points to the undeniable fact that the Chilean's verse and essays reflected the latest European achievements in poetry and aesthetics and initiated corresponding trends in Latin America. [4] Although there was no formal school or banner for Creacionist poets, its influence was manifest in poets such as Pablo Neruda, Jorge Carrera Andrade, Oliverio Girondo and, as we will demonstrate later in this chapter, Carlos Pellicer.

Undurraga points out that the influence of Creacionism was paramount in the development of avant-garde poetry in Mexico.

---

[3] Poggioli, p. 73.

[4] For recent studies on Huidobro and Creacionism see works by Braulio Arenas, Bary, Roggiano, Sucre, Undurraga, and Videla which are included in the bibliography. In her impressive study of Ultraism Videla notes: "Dos hechos acaecidos en 1918 contribuyen a la aparición del ultraísmo en España. El primero, el paso del poeta chileno Vicente Huidobro por Madrid." (p. 25) Later she adds: "la creacionista es, sin duda, de todas las escuelas de vanguardia, la que dio a Ultra mayores aportes." (p. 101) In his summation of the importance of Huidobro Braulio Arenas states: "Impone la voz de nuestro continente en la polémica del arte moderno y de la poesía de vanguardia,..." (p. 41).

The theories of Estridentismo owe much to Futurism and Creacionism. The "Contemporáneos," especially Ortiz de Montellano and Salvador Novo reflect in their poetry the aesthetic doctrine of Creacionism, but it is Pellicer who is chief exponent of Creacionism in Mexico. Undurraga contends that "en Carlos Pellicer la influencia del Creacionismo de Huidobro es mucho más constante y perdurable." Later he adds: "Sin duda, que la de Carlos Pellicer fue una de las primeras tentativas de adaptar los aires creacionistas a una poesía simple y vernaculista." [5]

Although Huidobro's initial literary ventures were strongly influenced by the French symbolists and Modernism of Rubén Darío, as early as 1913 the Chilean poet began to realize the uniqueness of the modern epoch. In a letter to the literary editor of *El Mercurio* of Santiago de Chile (Nov. 15, 1913), he writes:

> Ahora estamos en otros tiempos, y el verdadero poeta es el que sabe vibrar con su época o adelantarse a ella, no volver hacia atrás. [6]

In a manifesto entitled *Non serviam* read in the "Ateneo" of Santiago de Chile in 1914 he states his desire to liberate art from Nature and to create autonomous realities:

> Hemos cantado a la Naturaleza (cosa que a ella poco le importa). Nunca hemos creado realidades propias, como ella lo hace o lo hizo en tiempos pasados, cuando era joven y llena de impulsos creadores. [7]

In 1916 Huidobro travels to Buenos Aires where he delivers his theories of Creacionism to the "Ateneo Hispano." He states that a work of art:

> es una nueva realidad cósmica que el artista añade a la Naturaleza y que debe tener como los astros una atmósfera propia y una fuerza centrípeta y otra centrífuga. [8]

---

[5] Antonio de Undurraga, "Teoría del creacionismo," in Huidobro, *Poesía y prosa*, p. 37.

[6] Vicente Huidobro, *Poesía y prosa: Antología*, 2nd ed. Madrid: Aguilar, 1967), p. 20.

[7] Vicente Huidobro, *Obras completas de Vicente Huidobro*, Vol. II, ed. Braulio Arenas (Santiago de Chile: Zig-Zag Editores, 1964), p. 643.

[8] Huidobro, *Obras completas*, Vol. II, p. 661.

Later in the same discourse he contends that "la historia del arte no es más que la evolución del hombre-espejo hacia el hombre-dios." In other words, he traces the development of art from the Aristotelian concept of poetry as an imitation of nature (mimesis) to his own aesthetic theories expressed in the poem "Arte poética" where "El poeta es un pequeño Dios."

Towards the end of 1916 Huidobro arrives in Paris where he joins a magazine called *Sic* and later is a co-founder of the magazine *Nord Sud.* Members of "Nord Sud" included Huidobro, Pierre Reverdy, Max Jacob, Paul Dermée and Tristan Tzara, but the leader was, without a doubt, Guillaume Apollinaire.

The aesthetic kinsmanship shared by Huidobro and other members of "Nord Sud" is evident in the following statements. Speaking on the art of his time Pierre Reverdy says:

> Estamos en una época de creación artística en la cual se han creado obras que, separadas de la vida, vuelven a ella porque tienen una existencia propia fuera de la evocación o de la reproducción de cosas de la misma. [9]

In an essay on literary aesthetics published in numbers 4-5 of *Nord Sud* (June-July of 1917) he states:

> Crear la obra de arte que tenga su vida independiente, su realidad y que sea su propio objeto, nos parece más elevado que cualquiera interpretación fantástica de la vida real, apenas menos servil que la imitación fiel, la cual, por otra parte, no la alcanzarán jamás los que la buscan, únicamente porque será imposible identificar el arte con la vida real sin perderlo. [10]

The preceeding quote is a statement of the postulates and theories of Creacionism and could well have been from the pen of Huidobro.

Apollinaire himself gives great emphasis to the idea of poetry as creation when he writes:

> Poesía y creación son una misma cosa; no se debe llamar poeta sino al que inventa, al que crea, en la medida en que el hombre puede crear. [11]

[9] Huidobro, *Poesía y prosa,* p. 47.
[10] Huidobro, *Poesía y prosa,* p. 47.
[11] Huidobro, *Poesía y prosa,* p. 58.

Nineteen twenty-two finds the poet in Paris continuing his dif-
fusion of creacionist doctrine to the group of "Estudios Filosóficos
y Científicos del Dr. Allendy" where he defines a creacionist poem:

> Es un poema en el que cada parte constitutiva y todo
> el conjunto presentan un hecho nuevo, independiente del
> mundo externo, desligado de toda otra realidad que el
> mismo, pues toma lugar en el mundo como un fenómeno
> particular y aparte de los otros fenómenos. Este poema es
> algo que no puede existir en otra parte que en la cabeza
> del poeta: no es bello porque evoque cosas que se han
> visto y que eran bellas, ni porque describa cosas bellas que
> tenemos la posibilidad de ver. Es bello en sí y no admite
> términos de comparación. No puede concebirse en otra
> parte que en el libro. No tiene nada semejante a él en el
> mundo externo, hace real lo que no existe, es decir, se hace
> el mismo realidad. Crea lo maravilloso y le confiere una
> vida propia. Crea situaciones extraordinarias que nunca
> podrán existir en la realidad, y, a causa de esto, ellas deben
> existir en el poema, a fin de que existan en alguna parte. [12]

A synthesis of creacionist principles is found in a poem entitled
"Arte Poética" which Huidobro insists was first published in Buenos Aires in 1916 (prior to his involvement in *Nord Sud* thus
his claim to title of initiator of Creacionism). In free verse form
Huidobro outlines the technique of the new poetry and the role of
the creacionist poet:

ARTE POÉTICA

Que el verso sea como una llave
Que abra mil puertas
Una hoja cae; algo pasa volando;
Y el alma del oyente quede temblando.

Inventa mundos nuevos y cuida tu palabra;
El adjetivo, cuando no da vida, mata.

Estamos en el ciclo de los nervios.
El músculo cuelga,
Como recuerdo, en los museos;
Más no por eso tenemos menos fuerza:

[12] Vicente Huidobro, *Antología,* ed. Eduardo Anguita (Santiago de Chile:
Zig-Zag Editores, 1945), p. 261.

El rigor verdadero
Reside en la cabeza.

Por qué cantáis la rosa, ¡oh, Poetas!
Hacedla florecer en el poema;

Solo para nosotros
Viven todas las cosas bajo el Sol.

El Poeta es un pequeño dios. [13]

The "Arte poética" and other creacionist doctrines were not to
fall on deaf ears in Latin America. Earlier in this chapter we cited
specific poets who recognized the importance of Huidobro to the
development of the avant-garde in Latin America. Let us now
examine specific instances of Creacionism in the poetry of Carlos
Pellicer.

This study, as we stated earlier, does not choose to embroil itself
in the arguments either defending or negating Huidobro's claims to
originality. But the reader will note that some poetic elements introduced here as creacionist will be discussed in the succeeding chapters
and attributed to different sources. This is not to deny Huidobro's
contributions, but to suggest a simultaneous creativity. For Huidobro was only one of hundreds of poets who were seeking a new
poetic that would be capable of responding to the challenge of
language and reality in the modern world. Huidobro's theories are
similar in many ways to those put forth by other *isms*, but in as
many ways show original thought in postulating guidelines for the
poet of the twentieth century. We hope our initial chapter which
discussed the aesthetic inheritance of Carlos Pellicer demonstrated
that Latin American poetry of the late nineteenth and early twentieth century had no one hero, no one school, and no fixed point
in time. Philosophers and poets, as well as other artists, all took
part in the formation of an aesthetic, a view of reality and a vision
of man's role within that reality. Thus the poetic elements we will
term as creacionist are those that are consistent with Huidobro's
manifestos and his, as well as other creacionists', poetry. They are
not necessarily exclusive of, nor antagonistic to, other theories which
will be later discussed.

---

[13] Huidobro, *Obras completas*, Vol. I, p. 255.

B. The Poem

The Creacionist poem, as we have seen earlier in this chapter, is a creation in and of itself. It needs no external, *a priori* reality to give it veracity or validity. It creates situations which could never exist in any reality other than that of the poem.

In his study of the modern lyric, Hugo Friedrich states that a modern poem:

> aspira a ser una entidad que se baste a sí misma, cuyo significado irradie en varias direcciones y cuya constitución sea un tejido de tensiones de fuerzas absolutas, que actuen por sugestión sobre capas prerracionales, pero que pongan también en vibración las más secretas regiones de lo conceptual. [14]

Later he adds:

> Si el poema moderno se refiere a realidades —ya de las cosas, ya del hombre—, no las trata de un modo descriptivo, con el calor de una visión o de una sensación familiar, sino que las transpone al mundo de lo insólito, deformándolas y convirtiéndolas en algo extraño a nosotros. [15]

Saúl Yurkievich shares the above view of the relationship of reality to the poem when he says:

> El arte no se propone la reproducción exterior, documental, fotográfica, de la naturaleza, ni tiene por único objetivo expresar un presente demasiado circunscripto. Cada obra de arte posee en sí misma su razón de existir, su propia verosimilitud... [16]

Or as Huidobro put it so succinctly: "Un poema es un poema, tal como una naranja es una naranja y no una manzana". [17] Obviously

---

[14] Hugo Friedrich, *Estructura de la lírica moderna* (Barcelona: Seix-Barral, 1959), p. 15.

[15] Friedrich, p. 15.

[16] Saúl Yurkievich, *La modernidad de Apollinaire* (Buenos Aires: Losada, 1968), p. 16.

[17] Huidobro, *Obras completas,* Vol. II, p. 697.

Yurkievich and Huidobro here support what is commonly called the contextual theory of poetry which proclaims the self-sufficiency of the poem. "Arte poética" cited above, is Huidobro's expression in verse form of that same thesis.

Where in Huidobro this is a statement of aesthetic doctrine, in Pellicer it rises above a formalistic principle and characterizes a unique, personal vision of reality that is inherent and natural.

Pellicer's relationship to the world surrounding him has never been a passive one. In an interview with this writer he spoke of his first encounter with the sea:

> Y cuando tenía yo esta edad, seis años, mi madre me llevó por primera vez al mar. Y este viaje por el río de Tabasco hasta la orilla del mar fue mi primer contacto, que llamaría yo, violento, con la naturaleza. [18]

The experience as described above is not one of mere contemplation; but rather the "violent" act of interiorizing that aspect of external reality.

In *Colores en el mar,* his first book of poems, the sea is not copied or described in accordance to an *a priori* adherence to an exterior reality, but undergoes a transformation, a creation in Huidobro's terms in the imagination of the poet. At times it is a great orchestral arrangement:

> Sonata alternativa de adelante y andantino. Las notas que no surgen en perlas se cuajaron. Y el mar se desmelena tocando su diurno concierto matinal en sus gloriosos pianos. [19]

Later the sea is children bathing:

> Pareció que en el mar
> se bañasen mil niños (13)
> ... ...
> Las olas se estaban bañando (15)

---

[18] Unpublished interview with the author.

[19] Carlos Pellicer, *Material poético: 1918/1961,* 2nd ed. (Mexico: Universidad Nacional Autónoma de México, 1962), p. 14. All further quotes of Pellicer's poems will be from this edition with the page number given in parentheses.

But ultimately it is an object over which the poet has complete control.

The use of creacionist techniques is found in many poems and isolated images throughout the early production of Pellicer. Most notable among these are a group of poems entitled "Suite Brasilera" and a poem which we will transcribe in its entirety, "El sembrador":

> El sembrador sembró la aurora;
> su brazo abarcaba el mar.
> En su mirada las montañas
> podían entrar.
>
> La tierra pautada de surcos
> oía los granos caer.
> De aquel ritmo sencillo y profundo
> melódicamente los árboles pusieron su
>   danza a mecer.
>
> Sembrador silencioso:
> el sol ha crecido por tus mágicas manos.
> El campo ha escogido otro tono
> y el cielo ha volado más alto.
>
> Sembrada la tierra.
> Su paso era bello: ni corto ni largo.
> En sus ojos cabían los montes
> y todo el paisaje en sus brazos.   (134)

Here we have many of the characteristics of creacionista verse: destruction of spacial concepts; "En su mirada las montañas/podían entrar" also; "En sus ojos cabían los montes/y todo el paisaje en sus brazos"; the joining of two disparate elements in one image as in the following example where the noun "tierra" is joined with the verb "oía": "La tierra pautada de surcos/oía los granos caer"; and most important the concept of the poet (here represented as the "sembrador") as creator of reality: "El sembrador sembró la aurora".

C.   THE POET

As Huidobro states in "Arte poética" the poet "es un pequeño dios." He expands this concept when he states:

> El poeta hace cambiar la vida de las cosas de la Natura-
> leza, saca con su red todo aquello que se mueve en el caos
> de lo innombrado, tiende hilos eléctricos entre las palabras
> y alumbra de repente rincones desconocidos, y todo ese
> mundo estalla en fantasmas inesperados. [20]

Friedrich refers to this attitude as the "dictatorial imagination"
that is, a poetic imagination that has complete liberty in recreating
reality according to the laws of the poet and not some external
absolutes. He contends that:

> El poder de la imaginación iniciado a fines del siglo XVIII
> ha llegado en el XX a su plenitud. También la lírica ha
> llegado definitivamente a ser el lenguaje de un mundo
> creado por la fantasía, que va más allá de la realidad o
> incluso la destruye. [21]

In Pellicer the poet's autonomy is proclaimed early in his literary
career in a poem from *Colores en el mar* entitled "Estudio":

> Jugaré con las casas de Curazao
> pondré el mar a la izquierda
> y haré más puentes movedizos.
> ¡Lo que diga el poeta!   (29)

And in the fourth poem of "Suite Brasilera" he writes:

> Profundamente oblicuo, el aeroplano
> se retorcía y el paisaje entero
> era un acto glorioso de mis manos.
> Sin un solo recuerdo ni un deseo,
> como un dios, desdoblé los panoramas,
> ataviado de luz, leve de vuelo.
> ¡Y juré entre las nubes alzar una
>   montaña!   (80)

In "Las colinas" the poet-creator-god is a painter whose will it
is to:

> ¡Dibujar las colinas!
> Repartirles los ojos

---

[20] Huidobro, *Antología,* p. 247.
[21] Friedrich, p. 311.

y llevarles palabras finas.
Mojar largo el pincel; apartar neblina
de las nueve de la mañana,
para que el vaso de agua campesina
se convierta en alegre limonada.   (165)

This theme is again repeated in "Elegía":

Si yo fuera pintor
me salvaría.
Con el calor
toda una civilización yo crearía.
El azul sería
rojo
y el anaranjado
gris;
el verde soltaría en negros estupendos.   (119)

In the poetic world of Pellicer the wind possesses the ability to
change the color of the landscape:

Y el viento que mesaba las ágiles palmeras
le cambiaba al paisaje el color   (15)

The day becomes a celestial gambler:

El día jugó su as de oro
y lo perdió en tanto azul.   (16)

And night is depicted as:

la selva de vidrio en agua abierta   (221)

The sky is water that has decided to fly:

El cielo de los Andes
es una agua divina que se ha echado a volar.   (69)

His poetry creates a world of fantastic events and autonomous
images that defy literal interpretations:

Por la tarde vendrá Claude Monet
a comer cosas azules y eléctricas   (29)

La desnudez os ilumina
como un poco de piano en la noche   (107)

D. The Creacionist Image

Although the method of formulating a creacionist image is
limited only by the imaginative powers of the poet, we have found
four constants in the creacionist imagery of Pellicer: (1) the combination in one image of two disparate things, (2) destruction of
normal limitations, (3) representation of the abstract and intangible
by the concrete, and (4) the creation of unreal sensuous imagery.

1. Creation of Unreal [22] Sensuous Images

If one were to catalogue the most repeated phrases used by
critics to describe the poetry of Pellicer, they would most certainly
be "sensuous," "visual," and "plastic." Speaking of the early period
of Pellicer's production, Octavio Paz states: "Mucho de sus poemas
de esa época no son más que una prodigiosa sucesión de metáforas
e impresiones visuales y sonoras." [23] Manuel Antonio Romero sup-
ports the above statement when he writes: "Carlos Pellicer Cámara
inició su carrera literaria con la alegría de un adolescente que se
entrega a la fiesta de los sentidos." [24] Finally, we cite Alfredo Roggiano who points out that the sensuality of Pellicer's poetry is not
an end in itself:

> Sensibilidad abierta a todas las dádivas del hombre, la
> naturaleza y los objetos de la cultura, Pellicer recoge la
> visión plástica del modernismo más sonoro y estetizante,
> para hacer de lo accidental y visible una suma esclarecida
> de sustancias y ritmos interiores... [25]

---

[22] We use the term "unreal" to refer to images which are not attached
to any consideration of an *a priori* exterior reality.

[23] Octavio Paz, *Las peras del olmo,* 2nd ed. (Mexico: Universidad Nacional Autónoma de México, 1965), p. 100.

[24] Manuel Antonio Romero, "Carlos Pellicer, huésped de la tierra,"
América, 55 (February, 1948), p. 57.

[25] Alfredo A. Roggiano, *En este aire de América* (Mexico: Editorial
Cultura, 1966), p. 170.

Pellicer's poetry abounds in visual imagery which subordinates intellectual expression. His poetry is involved with the world of things rather than with metaphysical ponderings. It is not our purpose to reiterate here all that has been written about this aspect of Pellicer's poetry,[26] but we will, however, stress an aspect of this imagery that pertains to the modern era as a direct inheritance from Baudelaire: the creation of unreal sensuous imagery in its most common form, synesthesia.

As Amado Alonso states in his study of sensuous imagery in Pablo Neruda, synesthesia was employed by the romantic poets, but it was primarily the impressionist and symbolist poets that renovated this technique and expanded its poetic qualities.[27]

Commenting on the use of synesthesia in Baudelaire, Angelo Bertocci states:

> We see its significance especially with reference to music and "suggestiveness." For to have a perfume evoked by color or sound means to enjoy two sensations as well as their merging. It is to subordinate, but not to subject, one sense to the profound unity of all the senses...[28]

Synesthesia explores the relationship between different senses and the effect they produce in transmitting sensation to the mind by their interpenetration and coexistence in a perception.[29] As George Beal explains:

> Either the two sensations (from two spheres of the sensorium) create the same *attitude* or affective state in the writer, or, as some psychologists suggest, the sensations in question have the same force or stimulus and are therefore freely interchangeable.[30]

---

[26] See Teresa Ponce de Hurtado, *El ruiseñor lleno de muerte* (Mexico: Editorial Meridiano, 1970), pp. 153-161.

[27] Amado Alonso, *Poesía y estilo de Pablo Neruda* (Buenos Aires: Sudamericana, 1966), p. 299.

[28] Angelo Bertocci, *From Symbolism to Baudelaire* (Carbondale: Southern Illinois University Press, 1964), p. 86.

[29] Stephen de Ullman, "Romanticism and Synesthesia," *PMLA*, LX, 3 (September, 1945), pp. 811-827.

[30] George Denton Beal, *Modern Theories of the Metaphorical Mode of Expression*, Ph.D. Dissertation (University of Pittsburgh, 1949), p. 315.

The use of synesthesia is not in itself a modern characteristic. Expressions such as "raspy voice" or "soft eyes" or "sharp hearing" have existed in colloquial speech, as well as in poetry prior to the XIXth century. Certain combinations of senses within poetic imagery are, however, characteristic of the modern attempts to expand the limits of sensuous experience.

Alonso points out that sound has always needed other senses in order to be expressed. We have frequent examples of this in Pellicer — "Ruido oscuro" for example. The inverse of this, sound to describe other senses, appears with far less frequency and is characteristic of modern incursions into synesthesia. Thus in Pellicer we have examples of the visual given in terms of the audible:

> Nubes en *sol* mayor
> y las olas en *la* menor.   (13)

> El oleaje finge rumores de gacela
> perseguida   (17)

> Desde el avión
> la orquesta panorámica de Río de Janeiro
> se escucha en mi corazón   (78)

> La bahía, dirigida como una orquesta
> toca las luces   (81)

> La luz, rota en el ritmo de la hélice,
> humeaba de furor entre mis ojos
> y se oía pasar.   (79)

In the last image light is not only described in terms of sound but is also given physical mass by virtue of the verb "rota."

A quite uncommon use of synesthesia is found in "Mi sed amarga que alzó gritos" where the sensation of taste is expressed in terms of sound, or the combination of smell and sight in:

> Es la bolsa de semen de los trópicos
> que huele a azul en carnes madrugadas
> en el encanto lóbrego del bosque.   (257)

In "amarillenta voz de radio" (125) he joins two sensations with a similar attitude, the feeling of brightness, linked in an audiovisual experience. The practice of joining two sensations sharing a

common attitude is repeated in: "Y ardimos en la sed del He-
lesponto." (150)

Other sensuous images are created by describing sound in terms
of touch which in turn is described in terms of light which is then
qualified by the word "ámbar" which has properties of smell and
light: "Tu voz tenía el tacto de las luces del ámbar." (221) One
can appreciate the ingenuity of combining four sensations within an
image, but its effect is limited by the obvious strain of the relationships.

The unreal sensuous image is not limited to synesthesia. For
example, movement is described in terms of color:

> El agua se mueve en semitono   (79)

An important use of sensory images in Pellicer is attaching
sensory qualities to emotive or physical states. Solitude is given
both dimension and sound in the following image:

> ruido de las vastas soledades   (258)

Absence is described in terms of taste and given a characteristic of
physical mass:

> tu dulce ausencia me encarcela   (335)

Thus the effect of sensuous imagery in Pellicer is multiple: it
can expand the sensuous limits of a given object by the introduction
of new senses; it can assign sensuous qualities to abstracts and
intangibles; or create what Friedrich calls "irrealidad sensible" [31]
in which real objects of nature become unreal through attachment
to a sensuous image.

2. Destruction of Normal Spacial and Temporal Limitations

Perhaps the single most important technical advancement of the
XXth century which altered man's vision of reality was the inven-
tion of the airplane. The once massive and imposing reality of
Nature was now seen in miniature from above. Tall mountains were

---

[31] Friedrich, p. 309.

now lumps of rocks, huge rivers were now but mere lines, large cities were but quadrangles on the terrain. The poet in capturing this new vision of reality certainly felt himself to be "un pequeño dios." Guillermo Sucre, in an article on the poetry of Huidobro, speaks of this desire of flight in his early verse:

> Toda la primera poesía de Huidobro está dominada por este rapto del movimiento, por esta aspiración al espacio y la liberación del aire. Para ello se crea su propio mundo. [32]

Very early in his poetic career Pellicer made a trip through Latin America and viewed this continent from a plane for the first time. The result of this trip was his second book of verse entitled *Piedra de Sacrificios* which contains a series of aerial poems entitled "Suite Brasilera." In images from these poems we can experience the new perspective of reality which is a result of aviation and the consequential destruction of normal spacial limitations:

> El cielo en mi frente
> cambiándome el mar.   (77)

> Tu mar y tu montaña
> — un puñadito de Andes y mil litros de
> Atlántico.   (79)

> El mar se baña entre mis brazos.   (80)

> Canción de las palmeras sobre la colina
> y de la colina junto al corazón.   (82)

This device is not only used in the poems of aviation but is also effective in expressing the closeness of two lovers:

> Tan cerca estás de mí
> que la estrella del ángelus nace entre
> nuestras manos.   (221)

Or it can express the strange perspective of a ship sailing at night:

> El buque ha chocado con la luna.   (320)

---

[32] Guillermo Sucre, "Poesía del espacio," *Imagen,* 43 (February 15-28, 1969), p. 7.

Once the borders of normal spacial confines are crossed the poet is free to attack even a more sacred absolute — time. Pellicer lives in two temporal worlds: one which is modern and Western in which time and history are linear, thus constantly moving to some end; the other is of his native tropical Tabasco and a circular concept of time characteristic of the precolumbian cultures of that region. In "Estudios" from *Hora y 20* he captures the essence of timelessness:

> Relojes descompuestos,
> voluntarios caminos
> sobre la música del tiempo
> ... ...
> La juventud se prolonga diez minutos
> ... ...
> las horas se adelgazan;
> de una salen diez.
> Es el trópico,
> prodigioso y funesto.
> Nadie sabe qué hora es.
> ... ...
> No hay tiempo para el tiempo.

He ends the poem with an image of time which is not speeding to some conclusion, but rather moves slowly in a circular path:

> Y en una línea nueva de la garza.
> renace el tiempo,
> lento, fecundo, ocioso,
> creado para sonar y ser perfecto.   (193)

3. *Combination of Two Disparate Elements*

Referring to the effects of the modern "dictatorial imagination" Hugo Friedrich states:

> Lo que en la lírica antigua era posible, pero poco frecuente, en la lírica moderna se ha convertido en ley: la paradoja de destruir relaciones materiales o encadenamientos lógicos suprimiendo las conjunciones para relacionar cosas y acontecimientos que no tienen nada que ver entre sí. Estamos en el reino fantástico de la imaginación. [33]

---

[33] Friedrich, p. 315.

In Huidobro examples of this "dictatorial imagination" can be seen in the images below which combine two disparate elements:

> La luna y el reloj ("Luna o Reloj,"
> *Poemas Articos*)

> Y en el humo de mi cigarro
> había un pájaro perdido ("Égloga,"
> *Poemas Articos*)

Through the combination of two existing elements of reality, the modern poet creates a situation that is unlike any that can exist outside of his poem. Thus a sky can be filled with automobiles:

> El cielo se llenaba de automóviles (77)

Palm trees can go shopping:

> Las palmeras desnudas
> andaban de compras por la Rúa D'Ouvidor. (77)

And a city seen from an airplane is "un libro deshojado." (79)

Pellicer's combination of disparate elements in one image has various effects. It can be humorous as in:

> El Pao de Assucar era un espantapájaros (71)

or, by the use of a single verb, the commonplace is converted into a fantastic event:

> El maíz en la mazorca
> reía de buena gana
> ... ...
> El cielo de Tilantongo
> vuela en un pico de garza (352)

Through combination of disparate elements the poet makes a statement about modern reality as an element composed of both the natural and the mechanical coexisting equally:

> Bajo las ruedas de las montañas
> el mar moderno y resonante
> rueda lentamente sus antiguas máquinas

... ...
Y el puerto suntuoso,
liberal y tropical
entre grúas y palmeras en reposo   (81)

And:

Bajaron las palmeras
de las trescientas olas automóviles   (262)

By combining words of the modern technical world such as
"ruedas," "máquinas," "grúas," and "automóviles" with traditional
natural elements the technical terminology is lifted to poetic heights,
expanding both its meaning and the limits of poetry as well.

Although these images are delightful in their own right, they
have the power to describe an object beyond the limits of normal
adjectivation. To express his awe of an airplane motor he states:

El motor que perfora el aire espeso
algo tiene de bólido y de toro.   (77)

or:

El aire está en soprano ligero   (79)

and:

la voz, la silenciosa
música de callar un sentimiento   (268)

At times, however, the combination of disparate elements creates
an obscure and personal image that defies any attempt of interpretation:

Aquella luna del pueblo
con su piano y su esquina
donde acabó la aurora   (124)

And:

la luz es un fruto que devora el paisaje.   (124)

Pellicer's early involvement with this technique is manifest in
a poem from his first book, *Colores en el Mar,* in which the body

of the poem constitutes a series of arrangements of disparate
elements:

> Ayer se hundieron
> un barco holandés y el Sol.
> La medianoche ha quedado estancada
> en los astros mayores y en los pechos de amor.
> En la playa hay preguntas y luciérnagas.
> En el puerto sólo yo soy feliz.
> ¡Tu nombre me salva del mundo!
> ¡Divina palabra!
>
>   Silencio y abril.   (37)

Through this seemingly chaotic arrangement one can sense the
frivolity and youthful exuberance that Pellicer brings to poetic
creation. Nothing is too sacred or too commonplace for his imaginative manipulations. Octavio Paz captures this sense of joy in Pellicer
when he states: "Su poesía es una vena de agua en el desierto; su
alegría nos devuelve la fe en la alegría." [34]

The final category, representation of the abstract and the intangible by the concrete, could easily be discussed here but its frequency of appearance in Pellicer's poetry merits its own section.

4.   Abstract and Intangible by the Concrete

As we have stated before, the poetry of Carlos Pellicer is a
poetry of things. He is a man fascinated with every aspect of the
world that surrounds him. As Frank Dauster points out:

> Dado el concepto de una naturaleza dinámica susten-
> tado por Pellicer, sería muy raro que fuera poeta de natu-
> ralezas muertas. El universo tal como lo entiende él, im-
> plica necesariamente la participación del hombre. No puede
> ser éste un espectador pasivo, ni tampoco un especie de
> notario que todo lo ve y lo anota en un cuaderno de ejerci-
> cios de verso... Para él, poesía significa compenetración de
> hombre con la naturaleza. Una de las técnicas dominantes
> de toda su obra es la personificación de la naturaleza. [35]

---

[34] Paz, *Las peras del olmo,* p. 107.
[35] Frank Dauster, *Ensayos sobre poesía mexicana* (Mexico: Ediciones
de Andrea, 1963), p. 47.

Pellicer's command of his circumstances goes beyond personifying objects of nature to making concrete and visible the abstract
and intangible. This process Dauster calls "concreción" which he
defines as "el proceso de reducir a la existencia concreta lo abstracto
o lo que, por grande, le parece al poeta inasible." [36] Hugo Friedrich
contends that this stylistic technique is not uncommon among many
modern poets: "Otra ley estilística," says Friedrich, "que se ha con-
vertido casi en tópico consiste en situar a un mismo nivel lo tangible y concreto y lo abstracto." [37] This technique in Pellicer however, was not simply a borrowed innovation, but an act which
demonstrated his natural desire to express himself in visible or
other sensual terms. His poetry is not about things, but rather the
things created in a reality all his own. His poetry approaches the arts
of sculpture and painting. Replying to a question on the profusion of
plastic imagery in his poetry Pellicer says:

> Mi afinidad con los pintores es inmediata. Siempre he
> creído que la música es la expresión más importante de la
> poesía. Vienen después, en orden decreciente, la pintura y
> la palabra. Si admito que el color y la línea están más
> cerca de lo que escribo que la palabra, es fácil comprender
> por qué he vivido más próximo a los pintores que a los
> escritores. [38]

In "Elegía" he writes "Yo tendría ojos en las manos/para ver
de repente." Here he expresses the desire to see by touching and
feeling and not through a conceptual process. This desire is again
repeated in "Estudios Venecianos":

> (Como Santa Lucía,
> llevaba yo los ojos en las manos
> para ver de tocar lo que veía.)   (226)

In this poetic reality his personal emotions are given physical
dimension: solitude; "es olvido esférico de mi soledad"; (234)
"Vuelvo a tí, soledad, agua vacía,/agua de mis imágenes, tan
muerta,/nube de mis palabras, tan desierta"; (267) "ausencia/man-

---

[36] Dauster, p. 48.
[37] Friedrich, p. 315.
[38] Emmanuel Carballo, *Diecinueve protagonistas de la literatura del
siglo XX* (Mexico: Empresas Editoriales, 1965), pp. 193-194.

zana aérea de las soledades"; (340) "veo tu soledad cárcel abierta";
(212) or this personification: "la soledad está pensando/junto a la
ventana." (157)

Note how in the second example solitude is not only given a
concrete representation through its metaphoric relationship to water
and clouds, but the intensity and immensity of the emotion is heightened as well through its attachment to elements which are vast and
unfathomable.

Another emotion which is made concrete is happiness, "por el
rincón de un sollozo/paso la felicidad." (224); here not only is
happiness personified by the use of the verb "pasó," but "sollozo"
is given physical dimension in the metaphor "rincón de un sollozo";
and "vago borde de la dicha." (335) No emotion or concept is free
from Pellicer's poetic sculpture: sound, "tu voz...de perfil," (221);
the afternoon is capable of being cut, "El segador con pausas de
música/siega la tarde." (135); and night is personified in "La noche,
lentamente se desnuda/para dormir sobre mi corazón" (72). Even
the inverse is possible as in the following image where two tangible
objects are described in terms of an abstract: "ventanas y puertas
de alegría" (29).

This then is the body of the poetic work of Pellicer. A world
of things, visible and invisible, but all transformed to correspond
to his unique vision of reality. Although, as we have demonstrated,
Pellicer had adopted many of the creacionist techniques, philosoph-
ically there was a distance between him and Huidobro. Where in
Huidobro there is a tendency to reject nature, Pellicer's relationship to nature is one of harmonious coexistence. It is an inter-
change by which the sun, the sea, the wind provide him with
inspiration, and he in turn dresses them in imaginative colors and
forms.

Thus we come again to the problem of classifications — is Pellicer a creacionist poet? To the extent that he adopts many of the
creacionist techniques we would answer yes. However, Carlos Pellicer is clearly not an avant-garde artist. While he adopts many of
the devices and attitudes which originate in avant-garde movements,
he is not disposed to the avant-garde mentality. His poetic production begins at a time when the avant-garde frenzy of the first two
decades of the century had subsided. Not only could he be more
temperate in his view of the immediate past, but he could be

selective in regard to the avant-garde innovations he wished to adopt in his verse. Thus, he is at once a "contemporáneo," a creacionist, an "ultraísta," but most of all he is Carlos Pellicer.

We have explored briefly in this chapter Pellicer's experimentation with the poetic image. It is an image freed from the bonds of an absolute, exterior reality — an image whose meaning and reason for being must be found within it. In the final chapter we will address ourselves more completely to this aspect of his poetic art in a study of the metaphor, the heart of poetry, and Pellicer's most resplendent gift to posterity.

IV

THEMATIC DEVELOPMENT OF REALITY

In the conclusion of the preceding chapter we raised the question of the degree of Pellicer's participation in the initial avant-garde efforts of the twentieth century. In our discussion of the themes and visions of reality as they appear in his poetry, we will address ourselves more in detail to that question. We will observe that the major difference between the avant-garde and Pellicer lies not in language or technique, but rather in their vision of the modern era. This essential difference is most clearly expressed in their corresponding attitudes toward the role of tradition in this age, or as T. E. Hulme perceives the distinction, the difference between the romantic and the classical spirit in art.

In his essay "Romanticism and Classicism" T. E. Hulme identifies the advent of modern poetry as the end of romanticism and the revival of a classical spirit. It is a revival which consists of the triumph of fancy over imagination. His definition of the terms classical and romantic are rooted in their varying views of man. The basis of romanticism, for Hulme, is:

> that man, the individual, is an infinite reservoir of possibilities and if you can so rearrange society by the destruction of oppressive order then these possibilities will have a chance and you will get Progress. [1]

In the classical concept, however:

---

[1] T. E. Hulme, *Speculations,* ed. Herbert Read, 2nd ed. 1936, rpt. (London: Routledge and Keegan Paul, 1949), p. 116.

> Man is an extraordinarily fixed and limited animal whose nature is absolutely constant. It is only by tradition and organization that anything decent can be got out of him. [2]

Therein lies the distinction: for the romantic man is basically good and of unlimited potential, while for the classicist he is limited and disciplined by order and tradition. [3]

For Hulme the classical revival is the return of poetry from the shadows of the infinite to the light of the here and now. He wants to remove poetry from some higher reality and treat it simply as a means of expression. As he writes in "A Lecture on Modern Poetry": "I want to speak of verse in a plain way as I would of pigs: that is the only honest way." [4]

Hulme was not alone in his association of modern poetry with a classical revival. In Mexico we have the "Ateneo de la juventud," in particular the poetry of Alfonso Reyes and in France it is Apollinaire himself. Yurkievich points out that for the French poet the new spirit represented a return to the classical. But as he explains:

> No un neoclasicismo, porque en vez de copiar a la Antigüedad crea un arte original, que posee de común con el clásico su gusto por la nobleza, la gracia, la simplicidad. Ambos estilos comparten el mismo concepto de belleza. El artista contemporáneo no debe rivalizar con los modelos antiguos, sino tratar de renovar los temas y los procedimientos apoyándose en los principios esenciales de aquel gran arte. [5]

In spite of the continuity of the classical tradition in modern poetry as it is expressed in Hulme's essay and Yurkievich's evaluation of Apollinaire, what characterized the initial outbursts of avantgarde manifestos was not a sense of harmonious union of past and present, but a sense of liberation from the tradition and a euphoric dive into the present and future. As we saw in our discussion of

---

[2] Hulme, *Speculations*, p. 116.

[3] Hulme, *Speculations*, p. 117.

[4] T. E. Hulme, *Further Speculations*, ed. Sam Hynes (Minneapolis: University of Minnesota Press, 1955), p. 67.

[5] Saúl Yurkievich, *La modernidad de Apollinaire* (Buenos Aires: Losada, 1968), p. 49.

Huidobro, Creacionism was for him a totally new and modern concept of poetry, diametrically opposed to traditional values. Marinetti's choice of the term "futurism" to describe his movement speaks for itself. Estridentism in Mexico was an attempt to destroy the old idols and replace them with new poets whose voices carry a contemporary message. Stephen Spender terms this appeal of the present as "Realization" which he sets forth as the initial stage of modern literature. He explains:

> Realization is the primary gesture of modernism, the determination to invent a new style in order to express the deeply felt change in the modern world. Industrial towns, machines, revolutions, scientific thinking, are felt to have altered the texture of living. Everyday language and taste reflect these changes, even though the image they mirror is ugly. It is only art that remains archaic, forcing its ideas into forms and manners that are outmoded. Therefore artists have to learn the idiom of changed speech, vision and hearing, and then mould the modern experience into forms either revolutionized or modified. [6]

The principal aesthetic guidelines of this period are: that the modern age demands a unique and similarly modern idiom; art must express the new; art is no longer found in placid, rustic settings, but in the urban centers; poetry is free from considerations of decorum, meter and form; beauty and nature are no longer of a higher, transcendent reality, but are found in the simple things of life. These are but a few of the declarations proclaiming the liberation of poetry found in the manifestos of the multitude of *isms* which emerged in the early years of the twentieth century. Brooks points out that these poets made little attempt to conciliate their aims with traditions, but rather "tended to make the simplest sort of readjustment, that of flat rejection." [7] Much of this poetry was negative and was praised not so much for what it wrote, but what it did not write. This negative reaction to the past was both a natural step and a necessary one if twentieth century poetry was to find an idiom able to express its vision of reality. But the guide-

---

[6] Stephen Spender, *The Struggle of the Modern* (Berkeley and Los Angeles: University of California Press, 1963), p. 83.
[7] Cleanth Brooks, *Modern Poetry and the Tradition* (Chapel Hill, North Carolina: University of North Carolina Press, 1967), p. 69.

lines we mentioned above are not to be thought of as the ends of modern poetry. They are the initial efforts to find a means to express modern reality. Let us examine some of these tendencies in Pellicer with the purpose of demonstrating that in his work they do not serve as an end, but as a means of expressing a poetic vision quite distinct from the avant-garde groups.

A. A POETRY OF SIMPLE THINGS

As we stated earlier, his first book of poetry treats two traditional poetic objects, the sea and the sun. The poems avoid any notion of what the sea or the sun may represent or mean. They express the excitement and joy of experiencing these two natural phenomena. In the poem "Recuerdos de Iza" which describes a small village in the Andes, he tells us plainly not to search for some hidden meaning since:

> Aquí no suceden cosas
> de mayor trascendencia que las rosas   (53)

And in "Divagación del puerto" he declares:

> Eché al cesto del día
> los papeles de la eternidad.   (72)

Here he clearly rejects eternity and later explains that the knowledge he seeks is found in the reality of things that surrounds him:

> Porque mi América y el comunismo
> de Francisco de Asís
> revolvieron en el vaso de mi abismo
> mi principio y mi fin.   (72)

In the poem "Eternidad" he proclaims:

> Divina juventud, corona de oro,
> ventana al paraíso.
> ¡Te poseo total! (La muerte no figura
> en el reparto íntimo.)
> Oíd lo que cantan las musas:
> enciende la noche, ha muerto el destino.   (101)

The emphasis here is on life as the key to paradise — knowledge of death and destiny are no longer viable alternatives. The parody of Darío's "Juventud, divino tesoro" is made for an obvious distinction. Where Darío ends his poem with the line "Más en mía el Alba de oro!" which finds hope in a time after death, Pellicer clearly rejects that concept when he states: "La muerte no figura/ en el reparto íntimo."

In "Elegía délfica" his poetic intentions are unmistakable when he proclaims:

> Apolo ha muerto.
> Desnudad todas las cosas de la tierra
>   y del mar.
> Desnudad la nube hasta entonarla en lluvia,
> y el aire de su impalpabilidad.   (305)

Here Apollo, representative of romantic and symbolist poetry, is dead and gives way to a poetry which lays bare the things of the world. He concludes saying:

> ¡Apolo ha muerto! Cubrid las liras-hombres
> con la Noche desnuda que al pie de la
>   Aurora, danza.   (305)

The poet as "liras-hombres," an obvious reference to the romantic conception of the poet as a lyre which was played by the winds of nature, is laid to rest with Apollo. A new poet, a creator of reality, is now born.

Pellicer in these examples echoes the call of González Martínez to return to "el alma de las cosas." It is a poetry that is involved with the experience of things as they are, and not as representative of a higher, transcendental order. It is a poetry in which the poet and the reader simply see things without understanding them. The poetry of seeing is considered one of Pellicer's strongest achievements in Paz's introduction to *Poesía en movimiento:*

> Cada vez que leo a Pellicer, *veo* de verdad. Leerlo limpia los ojos, afila los sentidos, da cuerpo a la realidad. [8]

---

[8] Paz, *Poesía en movimiento,* p. 14.

Pellicer approaches reality not with the purpose of understanding it or abstracting it, but with the imagination of a child who simply enjoys seeing. As Baudelaire wrote: "Everything the child sees is *new*; he is in a constant *state of rapture*. Nothing more closely resembles what is called inspiration than the joy with which the child absorbs form and color." [9] This ability to see as a child was for Baudelaire a mark of genius:

> But genius is simply *childhood recovered* at will, childhood now endowed, in order to express itself, with virile organs and with an analytical mind that enables it to order and arrange all the materials accumulated involuntarily. [10]

Pellicer's poetry is replete with examples of "the joy with which a child absorbs form and color." In "Apuntes coloridos" he writes:

En una cuenca de los Andes
rápidos y hostiles,
se mueve un lago vibrante
dueño de islotes y dulces confines.

Muévense el verde y el azul
hasta tonalizar nuevos colores
y en los blancos clarísimos de espuma
hay difusión de flores.

En el cielo hay una danza de nubes.
El lago copia las mejores líneas
y las robadas sombras blancas
en la tarde se doran y se pintan.
Se torna el lago mágica acuarela
en las que formas toco y bebo tintas.

Azules crepusculares y ocres de agosto
míranse del otro lado.
La tarde con su estrella solitaria
abre un halo a los Andes solitarios.   (54)

This is but one aspect of the sensibility of modernity; let us look now to other expressions.

---

[9] Baudelaire, *Literary Critic,* p. 294.
[10] Baudelaire, *Literary Critic,* p. 295.

B. The Idiom of the Modern Age

This aspect of modern poetry has three manifestations: the creation of imagery which is contiguous with modern expression (covered in the chapters on creacionism and the metaphor); the introduction of traditional non-poetic vocabulary, in particular terminology and objects of the technical and mechanized world; and the inclusion of colloquial speech and conversational cadences in poetry.

There is no great preponderance of either of the last two elements in his poetry. His main technique to produce an effect of a conversation is the use of remarks in parentheses. They convey the feeling of immediacy, as if the poet were speaking to the reader while writing his poem, and they tend to disrupt the fixed, rhythmical cadence of the poem with an irregular conversational one. In "Las colinas" he includes a conversation between himself and a group of hills:

> Conversación.
> —Nosotras estamos aquí siempre.
> Nunca vamos a la ciudad.
> Estamos convencidas de la belleza
> del Ixtaccihuatl y el Popocatépetl.
> Cuando seamos grandes aprenderemos
> también a patinar sobre la nieve.
> —Pero si ustedes son más hermosas;
> son la sonrisa
> de mi caja de lápices. Ahora
> mismo me lo decían
> las palomas.
> La opinión de las águilas
> claro está que es muy otra.
> Pero esos zopilotes estandartes...
> Les envidio a ustedes la tarea
> de recoger las estrellas
> que quedan tiradas en la mañana.
> —Sí: tenemos ya una colección bastante completa
> Dicen que las pagan muy bien en Groenlandia.
>
> (164-165)

In "Semana Holandesa" he captures the conversation of Amsterdam in bits and pieces:

Nos veremos a las 7 en Kalverstraat.
No puedo porque voy a la Sinagoga.
Es falso; la reina no abdicará.
"Simplicissimus." "Il Secolo d'Italia."
"Izvestia." "The Times." "Sol y Sombra."
    "Le Journal."
"Izvestia." "The Times." "Sol y Sombra." "Le Journal."
Curazao, 1920! Nostalgias marino-comercial.   (181)

And in "Concierto breve" a whole poem is written in the form of
a dialogue:

    —La ciudad se construye cada vez menos.
    ¿Entiende usted?
    Pronto quedarán las ventanas
    con una mano pensativa.
    Días buenos, ve, con porcelanas sensitivas.

    —¿No hay peligro de estar?
    —El riesgo es de no estar puntualmente a la hora
    en que el sol nos reúne, lejos de él, a rezar.
    —¿Y los puentes?
    —Son preguntas sin respuesta.
    —Es verdad, como en Brooklyn, en Londres
        o en Marsella.

    —¿Y el loco? ¿No hay peligro?
    —Pintó la muerte de Nuestra Señora
    y asistió. Es loco de camino...
    Y cayó una de esas horas
    que hacia el reloj de Brujas moviliza
        el destino.   (246-247)

And in "Pausa naval" he introduces an expression that is not only
considered non-poetic, but approaches the vulgar:

    El mar en los cantiles de rincones
    entra a buscar sus muebles
    y derrumba los pianos apilados
    y los sofás enormes y las pailas
    y se va como entró gritando en grande:
    ¡al-carajo-al-carajo!   (263)

The inclusion of colloquial speech and conversational cadence is
not done at the exclusion of regular poetic rhythms or traditional

poetic vocabulary. Its use is not capricious nor merely striving for shock value. It is used when it is necessary to capture a moment or express an emotion, that would lose intensity with any other vocabulary or rhythm. It appears as an integral and necessary part of the poem expressing a particular vision, mood or rhythm of modern reality. It is in Pellicer a positive force where in some of the earlier practitioners, especially in the "estridentistas," it was used merely to dislodge poetry from a traditional metrical pattern and to shock the bourgeois reader.

The distinction between Pellicer and some of the early avantgarde poets is more vividly illustrated in his use of technical terminology and objects of the mechanized world. Where the futurists and "estridentistas" eulogized velocity, the machine, and other technical elements of the modern age, we see in Pellicer an integration of modern terminology in a harmonious relationship with more traditional poetic elements:

> América, América mía :
> desde al alarido del salvaje
> hasta la antena de radio-telegrafía.
> Desde la selva sin sendero y el camino
>   pastoril por la sierra
> hasta la locomotora y el hidroavión ;   (63)

and ;

> ante ti el motor de mi ser centuplica
> la libertad heroica de sus ansias
> y enciende la voz del olvido
> sobre sus horas trágicas.   (67)
> ... ...
> Bajo las ruedas de las montañas
> el mar moderno y resonante
> rueda lentamente sus antiguas máquinas.   (81)

We see here that the modern vocabulary is not served by the poem, but rather enhances the effect of a particular image. Nowhere in his poetry do we find an adoration of the machine. The airplane, although a frequent element in his early poems, is not eulogized, but treated as a means by which the poet is given a unique and new perspective of reality. In practice, Pellicer's treatment of the mechanized and technical world, quite distinct from many avant-garde poets, is a criticism and negation. As we will see later, machines and other technical manifestations are negative elements of a life style which he abhors and replaces with an alternate one. But prior to discussing that particular element in his poetry, let us attempt to resolve the obvious question raised by Pellicer's apparent contradiction of an idea of modern poetry.

C. TRADITION IN PELLICER

How can the futurists, the estridentistas, and Pellicer, all be classified as modern poets? Certainly there must be more than historical proximity. Stephen Spender offers the solution in his essay "Moderns and Contemporaries." "The contemporary," says Spender:

> belongs to the modern world, represents it in his work, and accepts the historic forces moving through it, its values of science and progress. By this I do not mean that he is uncritical of the world in which he finds himself. On the contrary, he is quite likely to be a revolutionary.... The contemporary is a partisan in the sense of seeing and supporting partial attitudes.... The contemporary is involved in conflicts, but fundamentally he accepts the forces and the values of today which are fighting one another, with the same weapons of power, ideology and utilitarian philosophy, for different goals. [11]

The characteristics clearly refer to writers and movements which made up the artistic avant-garde of the early twentieth century. In Spender's opinion these writers, although they are clearly contemporary, do not represent the modern spirit. "The modern," continues Spender:

> is acutely conscious of the contemporary scene, but he does not accept its values. To the modern, it seems that a world of unprecedented phenomena has today cut us off from the life of the past, and in doing so from traditional consciousness.... The modern is the past become conscious at certain points, which are ourselves living in the present.

---

[11] Spender, p. 77.

Hence we find that the modern in his work is occupied with trying to bridge a gulf within his own awareness, of past from present. With his sensibility he is committed to the present; with his intellect he is committed to criticizing that present by applying to it his realization of the past. [12]

C. M. Bowra points out that the modern poet who claimed to express a contemporary consciousness ran a risk due to the ambiguity of the term "contemporary." As he points out:

it may refer not to modern life as a whole but to those qualities in it which distinguish it from the past, and it is but a small step from this to a false view of the contemporary consciousness. [13]

He uses the Italian futurist, Filippo Marinetti to illustrate his contention. "Marinetti," says Bowra:

believed that a new art of words, which played havoc with grammar and punctuation, would give a wonderful force to the human spirit, and reflect the dynamic modern world. He felt that poetry was stifled by the past, and proclaimed his "horror of what is old and known" and his "love of the new and unforeseen." He believed that since we live in an age of machines, we find our self-expression through them and have developed a new kind of mind. [14]

But the narrow logic of Marinetti which excluded the whole past and the poetic tradition gave an inaccurate and unsatisfying, as well as an incomplete, vision of modern reality. As Bowra concludes: "Marinetti was deluded by his myopic view of what life today really is." [15]

The poetic vision of Marinetti, of the "estridentistas" and other avant-garde movements, while predominant in the early part of the twentieth century, was certainly not unanimous in its appeal. A less revolutionary attitude and vision, which was more conciliatory in its treatment of tradition, eventually triumphed.

---

[12] Spender, p. 78.
[13] C. M. Bowra, *The Creative Experiment* (London: Macmillan, 1949), p. 14.
[14] Bowra, *The Creative Experiment*, p. 14.
[15] Bowra, *The Creative Experiment*, p. 15.

It was manifest in a spirit which feels uncomfortable in a world run by the clock and controlled by the machine, a world which diminishes man to an ineffectual particle. In response to a literature which eulogized the present, we see a literature rich in universal significance and nourished by religious and literary traditions not only of Europe, but of Africa, Asia, and precolumbian America. Ezra Pound in his Cantos recalls the wealth of Chinese, Provenzal, ancient Greek and Italian lyrics. Tablada introduces the "haiku" to hispanic literature. T. S. Eliot returns to his Anglo-Saxon heritage for many of his symbols. Alfonso Reyes makes vital and relevant the rich literature of the ancient Greeks. This return to tradition is not a categorical acceptance of the past, nor a return to a belief in a chronological historical progression. Tradition now acquires a new character, a more universal and atemporal significance. As Ezra Pound reveals:

> The tradition is a beauty which we preserve and not a set of fetters to bind us. This tradition did not begin in A.D. 1870, nor in 1779, nor in 1632, nor in 1564. It did not begin even with Chaucer. [16]

It is a return to a time outside of history, a return to origins. Pound continues:

> A return to origins invigorates because it is a return to nature and reason. The man who returns to origins does so because he wishes to behave in the eternally sensible manner. That is to say, naturally, reasonably, intuitively.... He wishes not pedagogy but harmony, the fitting thing. [17]

Pound, as we can see, is not talking about tradition in a strict sense as some historical past which is chronologically connected to the future, but a tradition which is in Spender's terms, "eclectic" in character. This for Spender is the "revolutionary concept" of tradition which he defines as "the introduction, into certain works, of critically selected traditions." [18] This attitude toward tradition is

---

[16] Ezra Pound, "The Tradition," in *Literary Essays of Ezra Pound*, ed. T. S. Eliot (Norfolk, Connecticut: New Directions, 1954), p. 91.
[17] Pound, p. 92.
[18] Spender, p. 91.

what divides the contemporary, whose exclusion of the past gives an incomplete vision of modern reality, from the truly modern poet. As he contends:

> The vision of a whole modern world — a whole fatality — related to a past which is also whole, if only in not being modern, is, let me emphasize again, essentially the characteristic of the modern. [19]

Within this concept of the modern, the poet has complete freedom to select or reject any tradition in his search for a complete vision and expression of his reality.

Brooks is in agreement with Spender when he states that the problem for the modern artist was "a choice between the raw, unqualified present, and the dead past." Those who avoided the dilemma were able to successfully weld past with present. [20] The confrontation of the present with the past is the modern situation, says Brooks, in which: "we are obsessed with a consciousness of the past which drives us back upon history in a search for meaning . . . ." [21] Let us turn to Pellicer and examine how this confrontation is presented and resolved in his poetry.

D.   ATTITUDES TOWARD THE MODERN ERA

As we demonstrated earlier in this chapter, Pellicer has most of the notable exterior trappings that have been identified with modern poetry. The notable difference between their appearance in the early avant-garde poetry and in Pellicer is one of attitude. Where in the first there is a tendency to revere these elements as true representatives of the modern spirit, especially in their opposition to previous poetic themes and techniques, in Pellicer they are not set apart, but integrated into an expression of a modern reality as a whole. Far from celebrating the mechanistic character of modern life (with its resultant off-shoots: urban life, capitalist oriented societies, mass-man, etc.), his poetry is a criticism of that sense of the modern. In "Divagación del puerto" he writes:

---

[19] Spender, p. 94.
[20] Brooks, p. 75.
[21] Brooks, p. 86.

Es claro:
me gusta más Veracruz,
que Curazao.
Aquí llega la primavera
en buque de vapor
y allá en barco de madera.
Y con la primavera
el amor. (74)

Later in the same poem he treats New York, an embodiment of
modern life, with a whimsical disdain:

Nueva York se opuso a mi conciencia
pero esta invaluable ciudad,
inclusos Rockefeller y Roosevelt,
por cinco centavos la pude comprar.
¿Verdad, Mr. Woolworth? (74)

Paris, another Mecca of the modern era, is given equally humorous
and unimpressive treatment. In this capital of the cosmopolitan
spirit and haven of art, all that impresses Pellicer is the lack of
sunshine:

Media hora de sol pinta la aldea
sin galos que es París.
30 minutos para vivir, y nada más. (189)

or its pallor in comparison to the sun of his native tropics.

Sol parisiense,
Sol bibliotecario y sacristán,
ve a jugar a la América
en los muros astronómicos de Uxmal. (194)

Pellicer's criticism is most strongly expressed in *Piedra* . . . .
where he laments the present state of the Latin American people.
In "Oda a Cuauhtémoc" he states it clearly:

Toda nuestra América vanidosa y absurda
se está pudriendo. (97)

He objects to the unfulfilled dreams of a unified Latin America and
the virtual selling-out to North Americans:

> Como en el reinado de Moctezuma,
> vendrán hombres blancos,
> y será por el Norte.
> ... ...
> Con sus fonógrafos y sus manos ladronas,
> su religión modesta y sus catálogos,
> y organizados por un dentista
> vendrán los bárbaros.   (90)

A most evident criticism of the modern aspects of life is in the general absence of favorable discussion of its obvious representations such as machines, speed, scientific and technological achievements, etc. A notable exception is found in the poem "Estrofa Neoyorquina" in which the poet is filled with awe and admiration of this massive urban center. But even here it is brought down to a natural level when he says "Tus edificios suben como los árboles del trópico." (217)

An examination of the poetic form in Pellicer's works reveals a criticism of early avant-garde attempts to replace traditional metric, rhyme and stanza schemes with a totally free system of versification. Although Pellicer demonstrates his ability to handle both free and blank verse, this is not done at the expense of traditional, regular and rhymed forms. The free verse form of "Elegía ditirámbica" coexists harmoniously with the traditional sonnet form. Regular tercets in hendecasyllables are violated, not merely to break with the traditional form, but rather to present a line faithful to the poet's desired expression:

> Y porque soy miseria y porque grito
> pronto de voz y de esperanza, y vengo
> pálido de mirar el infinito,
> te saludo.   (212)

Pellicer is open to all forms for his poetry from traditional hispanic meters, to new ventures into free verse, to traditional foreign forms such as the "haiku." [22] Although there are many examples of the "haiku" in Pellicer's poetry, most notable are, "Recuerdos de Iza" and "Estudio" in which he writes:

---

[22] For a complete study of the haiku in Mexican poetry see, Gloria Ceide-Echevarría, *El haikai en la lírica mexicana* (Mexico: Ediciones de Andrea, 1967).

3. Las casas juegan a la buena suerte
   y la niña de quince años
   inocente como la muerte.

4. Hay una sed de naranja
   junto a la tarde todavía muy alta.

5. El agua de los cántaros
   sabe a pájaros. (218)

We are not going to attempt a prolonged study of poetic form in Pellicer listing the number of poems employing modern forms as opposed to those using traditional meters and rhyme schemes. Such a study would lead to this conclusion: Pellicer's choice of form is not determined by a premeditated plan to be either regular or irregular, traditional or innovative, but is determined by the demands of the particular poem. If what he wishes to express is best accomplished by a regular form then that will be his choice. Likewise some expressions need free rein, and that is not denied them. The poem determines its form rather than *a priori* judgment on the values of traditional and modern metric forms. In this particular area of poetic form Pellicer demonstrates his ability to reconcile past and present, the new and the traditional. He uses or rejects a form because of its appropriateness or inadequacy, not because it is traditional or modern.

Let us examine more closely the presence of tradition in his work, not as an eclectic process, involving themes and techniques, but as a program which establishes an alternative to modern life by what Spender calls a "pattern of hope." Spender discusses six programs of techniques by which modern literature and art express modern reality as a whole vision of "past-future confrontation." The second category or program he classifies as "pattern of hope" which is "the idea that modern art might transform the contemporary environment, and hence, by pacifying and ennobling its inhabitants, revolutionize the world . . . ." [23] In Pellicer we see this idea emerge in two distinct forms: the first is a short-lived political poetry, a blend of apologetic and didactic statement, on the failure of Latin America to live up to its historical past and potential; the other is more personal, expressing a need for reconciliation with

---

[23] Spender, p. 84.

the past and tradition to enable him to understand and cope with a chaotic present.

Piedra de Sacrificios was written by a young and extremely idealistic Pellicer. Active in government and student groups, and recently returned from a trip through Latin America during which he witnessed some despotic governments, Pellicer launches his book of poetry to awaken the spirit of his fellow Americans to present failures, past glories and future promises.

The initial poem of the book is an ode which enthusiastically sings of a united Latin America without artificial national boundaries. He calls forth and praises the heroes of its past, both Latin American and Spanish:

> Frescas herencias de hombres de diamante
> fructificarán.
> Cuauhtémoc, jóven y heroico,
> Atahualpa y Caupolicán.
> Bolívar y San Martín,
> y Pedro emperador del Brasil
> y Sucre y Morelos y Juárez
> y Artigas y Morazán y José Martí.
> Loadas sean España y Portugal;
> la espada del Cid y las brújulas de Colón
> y de Vasco de Gama.   (64)

He recalls the richness of Latin America, both in its human and natural resources. And closing on an optimistic note he calls to Latin America to reap its future harvests:

> América, América mía,
> loada sea esta alegría
> de izar la bandera optimista.
> Cúmplete a ti misma tus cosechas futuras,   (65)

The following poem "Uxmal" which we discussed in an earlier chapter revives the glorious precolumbian past as part of the heritage that will carry Latin America to future glories. [24] Other

---

[24] We are not going to discuss in depth the elements of the indigenous cultures in Pellicer's poetry since that theme was treated fully in Francisco Pavon's study, *Gravitación de lo indígena en la poesía de Carlos Pellicer.* See bibliography.

poems are dedicated to various natural phenomena of Latin America. But in poem "14" his tone changes from optimism to rage:

> Y los ojos se me llenaron de odio
> pues junto a mí estaba el cadáver del
>   Libertador
> de América. Los déspotas nativos negáronle
>   sepulcro
> y se pudría bajo el magno ojo del sol.   (83)

Bolívar, another of the great inspirational heroes of Pellicer, even in his lifetime saw the hopes of a united Latin America shattered. The present state of affairs lent no solace to his soul. In the closing lines Pellicer denounces those who have forgotten the ideals of the Liberator:

> Tierras de América estranguladas por los
>   déspotas,
> o por el yanqui, líder técnico del deshonor.
> La indiferencia sombría de vuestros hermanos
> no detendrá el aerofuego fraternal del sol,
> el instante de una bolivariana aparición.   (84)

In a poem entitled "Cuba" the political nature of his protest bursts forth in anti-Yankee sentiment:

> Te estranguló con mano higiénica
> el yanqui cínico y brutal.
> Civilizáronte y perdiste
> tifo, alegría y libertad
> Cuba divina,
> tierra naval y bailarina,
> entre el danzón de tu apodo
> corre la sombra de tu ruina.   (88)

And in a tone mixed with cynicism and despair he declares that Latin America's consolation will come in the afterlife:

> Nuestra América parecía
> que entre sus árboles se suicidaba.
> Y El vio nuestra angustia, nuestro oscuro
>   llanto;
> nos vio serenamente cara a cara.
> Sobre nuestros hombros colocó sus manos;

bienaventurados los que sufren, dijo,
porque ellos serán consolados.   (91)

In "Soledad" the tone shifts from despair to one of mild outrage:

¡Hasta cuándo mi vida
ha de ser solamente una ala presentida!   (92)

It is an outrage at potential that becomes nothing more, but more
an outrage at his position of solitary despair. But at the end of the
poem he promises that his silence is about to end:

Aguas del corazón, aguas vencidas
que votaron la paz para mi corazón.
Os habrá de agitar esa ala presentida.
Quebrará con sus plumas los vidrios de la paz.
¡No sé!... ¡Pero este vasto silencio
   de mi vida
anuncia un grito largo, un gran grito de
   mar!   (93)

In the final poem of *Piedra...*, "Oda a Cuauhtémoc," Pellicer
presents his "pattern of hope," his plan for change. The first part
of the poem recalls the history of Cuauthémoc, last of the Aztec
"Tlacatlecutlis," and the tragic conquest of his people until it reaches the final optimistic crescendo:

¡Oh Señor! ¡Oh gran Rey! ¡Tlacatecutli!
¡Oh solemne y trágico jefe de hombres!
¡Oh dulce y feroz Cuauhtémoc!
¡Tu vida es la flecha más alta que ha
   herido
los ojos del Sol y ha seguido volando en el
   cielo!
Pero en el cráter de mi corazón
hierve la fe que salvará a tus pueblos.   (97)

The hope lies in faith. Faith that reminds him that the noble heroes
and glorious heritage are not part of a dead past, but one that is
constantly present. The answer is not to despair at the present in
lonely silence, but to reaffirm the commitment, to rediscover one's
true self, to revitalize the past into a plan of action for the future.
To put it simply, for Latin America to understand who it is and

where it is going, it must first realize who it was and where it had been.

As we stated earlier, the political and regionalist character of this form of expressing modern reality as past-future confrontation is short-lived. In fact it is confined to the book *Piedra de Sacrificios*. The second form of expression, which is at once more personal and universal in character, is a constant throughout his whole work and, in fact, represents the nucleus of his art.

Cleanth Brooks, in his discussion of John Crowe Ransom's poetry, offers an interesting insight into the dilemma of the modern. The dilemma is that of man's "divided sensibility." [25] As he explains:

> In the form most familiar to us, the division reveals itself in the contrast between the broken and confused life of the mature man and the innocent and total world of childhood which he has grown out of. [26]

The problem of the "divided sensibility" turns to desperation when man realizes that he can never hope to attain a "unity of being" and recapture the innocence and peace of childhood:

> Childhood — the childhood of a race or of a culture — gives a suggestion of what such unity can be, but development into maturity, and specialization, break up the harmony of faculties and leave intellect at war with emotion, the practical life with the life of sentiment, science with poetry. [27]

Despair is one response to the modern's predicament, but it is not the only one and certainly not the one Pellicer expresses.

We demonstrated earlier that Pellicer's attitude toward modern life in its mechanistic, scientific and social manifestations, ranges from bewilderment and indifference to utter disdain. He is a man out of compass with time in a strange environment. Modern urban centers, rather than impress him, make him aware that he is a foreigner and recall images of his native land. He is a man alone in constant search for meaning, seeking a reunion, hoping to regain

---

[25] Brooks, p. 88.
[26] Brooks, p. 89.
[27] Brooks, p. 90.

a harmony and peace he once knew. Two interrelated themes pass dialectically throughout his early poetry: that of solitude which is a result of a lost unity; and, travel.

Early in *Colores* . . . he writes:

> Pasé todo el día pensando en sus manos.
> ¡Tan amantes sus manos de amor!
> Provincia. Paisajes lejanos.
> Dolor.
>
> Mi llanto de niño de entonces . . .
> La noche de luna de la despedida . . .
> Nuestras manos henchidas y ansiosas
> llenaron la vida.   (35)

Here is the first instance in which the poet recalls a past time, a lost childhood, whose pleasant memories bring him sadness because they are only memories. The political involvement of *Piedra* . . . offers some reprieve, but that is fleeting. In "La Noche" he writes:

> Bajo la dulce penumbra
> de la noche de luna de la ausencia,
> canta el poeta su tristeza.   (104)

A sense of loss is evident is "Soledades" a poem which gravitates around the repetition of the verb "recuerdo" and ends:

> Sólo por ti estoy despierto
> en esta media noche
> de mi desencanto universal.   (109)

These final three lines are important because they demonstrate the universal character of his solitude. Most of the poems in which the theme of absence and solitude appear could be interpreted simply as love poems bemoaning the separation of two lovers. But there is a tone in these poems that carries the feeling beyond that interpenetration. We rarely sense the lover as a person. The lover is a motif which introduces the theme of solitude in a cosmic sense. It is not the solitude that comes as a result of the absence of a lover, but that which comes with the loss of an age, a time of innocence and happiness. It is this time, this instance that he recalls in "Nocturno":

¿Recordáis ese minuto heroico,
cuando el universo se os derrumba en lágrimas
y un sólo acto de ternura
os pone en pie sobre las ruinas
izándonos el alma?
... ...

Por ese instante luminoso
que abarca el ritmo universal
y nos entrega, fugazmente,
una estupenda fe de crear.

Por ese instante, que un instante
fuimos capaces de sentir
y un trigo ideal sembró la mano
y en labios de oro fue el decir.   (129)

The theme of travel which appears throughout his poetry likewise transcends literal interpretation. Pellicer's journeys take him throughout South America, New York, Paris, Rome, Holland, Greece and the Middle East. He sums up his feelings for travel in the poem "Divagación del puerto":

Dulce melancolía
de viajar
Ilusión de moverse a otro poema
que alguna vez se había de cantar   (74)

and

¡Viajar!
Es una ilusión
más.   (75)

The travel Pellicer undertakes is more than a movement from one geographical locale to another. Its purpose is beyond adventure and excitement. Travel here is a temporal movement as well as a geographical one. It is a search for reunion with a lost age, a hope for restoration of harmony, a search that in most instances is little more than illusion. In "Variaciones sobre un tema de viaje" (dedicated to Alfonso Reyes) the illusion of travel is again repeated:

Pompeya, Atlantic-City de otros días,
rastacuera y feliz, regó su noche

de amor con el Vesubio, y cuál sería
la ida y la venida del asunto,
que, toda perla, la encontré quebrada,
las manos negras y los rizos juntos.   (148)

But upon arriving in Athens the tone changes to one of excitement
and hope:

Tardes de Atenas, ínclitos asuetos
cuyas perfectas horas me llevaban
los ojos grandes y los labios netos.

En mi reloj romántico cernía
la arena de sus playas el cuaderno
sonoro de mis viajes en que fía

la esperanza su fe de buen arribo,
su última onda, su primer pisada
y su deseo próximo cautivo.   (149)

At last he finds some meaning in travel. Athens is now not simply
a city, but a living, pulsating force which communicates to him.
The experience is repeated when he visits the Holy Land and
retraces the steps of the Saviour:

Y yo ví lo que Él vio. Mis pies pasaron
por donde Él caminó. Sueltos y reales
los lirios salomónicos alzaron

el himno al libre lujo de sus telas,
y la sombra olivar, agria y torcida
se cruzaba de pájaros.

Mi fe quemó sus piedras poderosas
como en todo lugar y el juramento,
luminoso huracán, me dio sus rosas.

Desos días
me quedó el corazón nuevo y humilde,
lento el pensar y los brazos cargados.   (151-152)

Travel here is no illusion. He reestablished the vital link, he seems
restored. The effect that Jerusalem and Athens have on the poet is
contrasted to that of the modern cities at the end of the poem when
he returns to France:

Nacen los muebles otra vez y crean
el universo igual que en sus estrellas rotas
nivelara perfiles agitados
bajo el agua mediocre de sus gotas. (154)

From the excitement and vitality he experienced in the presence
of timeless Athens and Jerusalem, he returns to the monotonous
everyday world of the present.

But why the search? Why suffer the pain that comes with
repeated failure and illusion? As we stated above, for some the
expression of the despair of separation and solitude would be suf-
ficient. Others might seek refuge in art or political commitment.
But Pellicer's character dictates another path. As he proclaims in
"La Primavera":

¿Qué sea el mundo un ataúd?
¡Qué sea! Pero con melodía
nuestra.
Y así tendremos ya caja de música
para danzar la danza maestra
de nuestra misteriosa inquietud. (102)

Pellicer is basically an optimist. His is an optimism born of
adherence to basic Roman Catholic traditions. He says it all very
plainly in the opening poem of *Colores* . . . :

En medio de la dicha de mi vida
deténgome a decir que el mundo es bueno
por la divina sangre de la herida. (9)

He has hope in the goodness of man and creation because of the
sacrifice of Jesus Christ. This simple statement of faith justifies
man's existence and gives it meaning. If modern man is unhappy,
alone, dehumanized, relegated to an obscure existence in the mechanistic cosmology of the modern world, it is because the life-giving
cord that connected him with the past was at some time severed.
Pellicer's poetry provides man with a means to reunite himself
with the past in order to have a meaningful present and future.
His vision of the modern world is not exclusively a near-sighted
present, but rather a total vision of the universe of past, present
and future. Pellicer's confrontation of present and past has three

major movements or forms of expression: Roman Catholicism; the precolumbian past; and Ancient Greece.

In the first, as we said, man, by the act of sacrifice, is given meaning and the promise of salvation and eternal life. This rather orthodox and simple affirmation of faith is remarkable if viewed within the context of religion's role in contemporary society. Barrett identifies the decline of religion as the "central fact of modern history in the West." [28] This is not merely a decline in popularity, but its displacement as the "uncontested center and ruler of man's life." [29]

Pellicer's faith goes back to the roots of Christian faith. It is, as Barrett says, "not only faith beyond reason, but if need be, *against* reason." [30] This simple but all powerful faith is captured in one of his "Sonetos dolorosos":

> Ordéname, señor, que yo te siga.
> Grítame, estoy muy lejos, no te veo.
> Me deslíe este largo veraneo;
> este afán de *no ser* da sólo ortiga.
>
> En donde a la belleza por amiga
> tengo, poca luz hay. Si te olfateo,
> las tempestades que capitaneo
> muelen la perla que tu pie prodiga.
>
> Y tengo que ir a Ti de un modo o de otro:
> a pie, en avión, locomotora o potro.
> ¿En dónde estás? ¿Por dónde está el camino?
>
> No sé qué voy a hacer cuando te vea.
> Que no sea un encuentro repentino
> para que así me luzca la tarea.   (529)

In his interest in the precolumbian past and Ancient Greece [31] he draws upon the pagan simplicity and harmony of those ages.

---

[28] William Barrett, *Irrational Man* (Garden City, New York: Doubleday and Co., 1962), p. 24.

[29] Barrett, p. 24.

[30] Barrett, p. 92.

[31] The influence of the Classics was certainly inspired by Alfonso Reyes as we pointed out earlier. Roggiano recognizes the importance of this aspect of Pellicer's poetry when he calls him a "clásico moderno." *En este aire de América*, p. 172.

Man's relationship to the land, the gods, the whole universe was a daily, reciprocal act. For all that man gave to the gods, he, in turn, received. The ages of Greece and Ancient America are recalled in a sonnet "En Atenas":

> ¿Por qué la mano lenta sobre el tambor
>   pulido
> desta columna rota, tórridamente va?
> Es la misma caricia con cierto aire de
>   olvido
> que deslizó sus dedos sobre Chi-Chen-Itzá.
>
> Y hay un viaje remoto que a un altar dividido
> dio su gozo y su espuma, sus esperanzas da.
>
> Y hay un retorno antiguo hacia un nuevo
>   sentido
> de Sol que abrió las cifras de Grecia y
>   Yucatán. (173)

This is a past not merely viewed as a dead time, but seen as a return, a vital and active force in the present. [32]

His poetry reflects the union of present and past as we have observed in numerous images which link modern day terminology with traditional poetic objects: the treatment of traditional themes in modern forms and colloquial language, but most important in the expressed desire to return the language of poetry to its initial stage, to recapture the real and vital rhythm of things, to write poetry that expresses things and not their abstract equivalences.

---

[32] His use of the past is in keeping with a tone of optimism that permeates his whole work. He goes beyond the defeat of his precolumbian ancestors to emphasize their greatness as a means to insure the continuing of goodness of man. The past is then an optimistic lesson to modern man whose being is splintered into fragments. It is an attempt to reconcile modern man and make him whole again. His involvement with the past is not marked by a desire to merely escape the present, but neither is it an attempt to create an exotic environment to replace sordid reality. It is a return to a past which is his own. It contains his beginnings, it is in fact, a recovery of this lost time in which he felt as one with the universe. This use of tradition in Pellicer represents the modern urge to find roots and reestablish a sense of identity with the distant past. His involvement with the precolumbian past has particular parallels with the resurgence of myth in modernity. See: John B. Vickery, "The Golden Bough and Modern Poetry," *The Journal of Aesthetics and Art Criticism*, XV, No. 3 (March, 1957), pp. 271-288.

His poetry seeks an alternative to the life style imposed by modern reality. In "Motivos" he turns to the simple life of the sheepherder:

> Pastor de las crías, tan tiernas
> que hay que acariciarlas,
> a veces la luna por ti está más cerca
> que tu propia casa.
> Al mejor paisaje le das tus becerros
> y en tus correrías,
> tu sed se ha secado con cuatro naranjas
> compradas al día.
> El día es tu feria, tu juguetería.   (116)

Two of his most brilliant creations are "Sembrador" and "Segador" where he likens the act of creating poetry to the simple acts of sowing and reaping:

> El sembrador sembró la aurora;
> su brazo abarcaba el mar.
> En su mirada las montañas
> podían entrar.
> ... ...
> El segador, con pausas de música,
> segaba la tarde.
> Su hoz es tan fina,
> que siega las dulces espigas y siega la
>   tarde.   (134 & 135)

In "Canción para una leyenda" he speaks of a time before time, a legendary, mythical time when there was a pure and simple relationship with life. It is a time when things were what they appeared without any deep transcendence when one could say simply:

> Eso nada más supimos,
> eso, y no más.   (136)

Through this world pass three travellers who are poets:

> Uno escuchaba el cielo, otro a sí mismo
> y el otro a todos los demás.   (136)

These three come upon three women in a tropical forest, but the simple beauty of that moment was lost and the poet asks:

¿Qué maleficio indestructible,
que satánica negación,
que absurda cita imprescindible,
atropellado por la razón,
echó a perder la virtud intangible
de nuestro dulce corazón?   (137)

He grieves the loss of viewing things simply and accepting a beautiful moment for what it is. But the poem does not end on a note of despair. In the final stanza the poet assures us that the light that guides the path to that simple time still shines:

Eran tres mujeres bellas,
La cabellera les daba hasta el pie.
Entre sus labios había una estrella
que aun ilumina sendero de tres.   (137)

Pellicer's desire to return to a time that was happier and simpler is not romantic escapism. He doesn't wish to escape the present, but rather he seeks ways of understanding it and surviving in it from lessons in the past. He desires not an escape to a time outside of time, but one within himself. His desire becomes his poetic. He seeks images that express things in a fresh manner. He battles with language to return it to some of its magical powers. We again refer to that most significant poem "Invitación al paisaje" where he writes:

De todas las ventanas, que una sóla
sea fiel y se abra sin que nadie la abra.
Que se deje cortar como amapola
entre tantas espigas, la palabra.   (186)

Let us emphasize again, Pellicer's poetry is an attempt to go beyond the word. It is an attempt to reach "el alma de las cosas." It is poetry which forsakes the name of things and captures their rhythm. This rhythm is felt in the ruined column of a Greek temple. It is seen in the movement of the stars. It is carried in the pulsation of the sea. He speaks of this rhythm that can be felt in all things in a poem dedicated to Tablada:

El sinfónico oído de colores
ha de escuchar un día
la melodía de otros horizontes.

> La mano que tocó todas las cosas
> ha de tocar un día
> proporciones sutiles, sombras de alas
>   gozosas.
>
> Y el brillo de la angustia sobre el alma
> ha de tornarse un día
> en mirada divina y en gozo sin palabras.   (196)

Even silence contains within itself a rhythmic force:

> Baila el silencio en la onda movida,
> buen bailarín
> en tonos libres y actitud oída.   (227)

But it is the tropics, the antithesis to modern life throughout Pellicer's poetry, from which the rhythm emanates most clearly and penetrates the being of the poet:

> La oda tropical a cuatro voces
> podrá llegar, palabra por palabra,
> a beber en mis labios,
> a amarrarse en mis brazos,
> a golpear en mi pecho,
> a sentarse en mis piernas,
> a darme la salud hasta matarme
> y a esparcirme en sí misma,
> a que yo sea a vuelta de palabras,
> palmera y antílope,
> ceiba y caimán, helecho y ave-lira,
> tarántula y orquídea, zenzontle y anaconda.
> Entonces seré un grito, un solo grito claro
> que dirija en mi voz las propias voces
> y alce de monte a monte
> la voz del mar que arrastra las ciudades.
> ¡Oh trópico!
> Y el grito de la noche que alerta el
>   horizonte.   (259)

The concept of rhythm in Pellicer is closely associated with his view of reality as flux to be discussed in the next chapter, but it is not synonymous to movement. Discovering the rhythm of things is going back to the beginning. It is coming into contact with pure, unnamed reality. Octavio Paz captures the idea when he says:

El ritmo poético es la actualización de ese pasado que es un futuro que es un presente: nosotros mismos. La frase poética es tiempo vivo, concreto: es ritmo, tiempo original, perpetuamente recreándose. Continuo renacer y remorir y renacer de nuevo. [33]

Pellicer is a significant poet of twentieth century Mexico not merely because he employs language, rhythms and images characteristic of modern poetry, but because his poetry is a total vision of modern reality. It is a vision which reestablishes the links among the present, past and future. His poetry demonstrates to man how to again live with himself and with his world by reviving those vital moments when man was truly free and communicated with the soul of all things.

---

[33] Paz, *El arco y la lira*, p. 67.

V

VISION AND EXPRESSION OF REALITY

In our discussion of Pellicer's vision of reality in this chapter we again broach the element of influence. To say that he was influenced directly or indirectly by some movement or writer is a delicate and tenuous assertion. To sustain that contention we might take recourse of the writer's own admission of said influence, rely on the statements of critics or seek to uncover the influence in the author's own works. Thus it is with no little fear of misrepresentation that we choose the philosophy and aesthetic of Henri Bergson to serve as the focal point of this chapter.

We choose Bergson for a variety of reasons which are enumerated below, but most importantly because his philosophy includes within it an aesthetic which corresponds to or directly influences poetic development in the twentieth century. [1] Whether Pellicer experienced Bergson firsthand, or through the work of José Vasconcelos (whose *Estética* is greatly influenced by Bergson) and other members of the "Ateneo" in Mexico is of little importance or

---

[1] Our estimation of Bergson is best summarized by William Barrett when he writes: "... the figure of *Henri Bergson* (1859-1941) cannot really be omitted from any historical sketch of modern existential philosophy. Without Bergson the whole atmosphere in which Existentialists have philosophized would not have been what it was. He was the first to insist on the insufficiency of the abstract intelligence to grasp the richness of experience, on the urgent and irreducible reality of time, and — perhaps in the long run the most significant insight of all — on the inner depth of the psychic life which cannot be measured by the quantitative methods of the physical sciences; and for making all of these points the Existentialists stand greatly in his debt." William Barrett, *Irrational Man* (Garden City, New York: Doubleday & Company, Inc. 1962), pp. 14-15.

consequence. What we wish to stress in our discussion is that the poetry of Pellicer is a vision of reality with roots in Bergsonian thought which rejects traditional views of reality and its representation, which consequently leads to a reevaluation of the function of art and the role of the artist.

Bergsonian philosophy is the metaphysical counterpart of the artistic reaction represented by symbolism and poetry of the new century. Marcel Raymond states the matter clearly in his study of the modern movement in French literature: "Bergsonism, which was auscultation of the self before it turned to the universe, seems to have developed along a curve parallel to that followed by the general development of literature in the same period." [2]

In order to understand and better appreciate the significance of Bergson's thought in the late 19th and early 20th centuries it is necessary to view the period in which it began. It was a period dominated by an adherence to empirical science as a means of explaining reality. Materialism, mechanism, finalism, positivism, Darwinism, tended to overpower metaphysical quests for knowledge by the brute force of mathematical formulas and scientific logic. Starkie recaptures the scientific mania that had gripped that period:

> The teachers at the Sorbonne had made light of moral problems; they had scorned religious experience, denied freedom and made idealism impossible. What is called the soul was reduced to the body; psychology was replaced by physiology; while evolutionary doctrine had been turned into a heartless assertion of natural selection, the struggle for life, and the survival of the fittest. [3]

In short, man was dehumanized, without will or spirit, differing only in degree from the rest of organic life. Bergson's philosophy is a challenge and repudiation of mechanistic and materialist theories as being not only insufficient in explaining reality, but by their concepts distorting a true vision of reality.

It is not the purpose of this discussion, nor within its scope, to discuss all the different elements and implications of Bergsonian

---

[2] Marcel Raymond, *From Baudelaire to Surrealism* (London: Methuen and Company, 1970), pp. 52-53.

[3] Enid Starkie, "Bergson and Literature," in *The Bergsonian Heritage,* ed. Thomas Hanna (New York: Columbia University Press, 1962), p. 79.

thought. This chapter will deal with those thematic and stylistic devices which appear in Pellicer that are congruous with Bergsonian philosophical attitudes.

Mexico, one of the first of the Latin American countries to introduce positivism, was also the first to mount a reaction against this philosophy which dominated the latter part of the nineteenth century. The spearhead of the attack on positivism was the "Ateneo de la Juventud" composed of notable figures such as Antonio Caso, Alfonso Reyes, Pedro Henriquez Ureña and Jose Vasconcelos among others. In his prologue to *Conferencias del Ateneo de la Juventud* Hernandez Luna examines some of the writers who influenced the course of the "Ateneo":

> Los autores y libros que leía y meditaba este grupo de jóvenes en sus pequeños cenáculos, y que al lado de la docencia de los maestros mencionados, influyeron para que se fuera apartando del positivismo, han sido confesados también por ellos. José Vanconcelos reconoce que las lecturas que influyeron en su grupo fueron ia de Schopenhauer, Kant, Boutroux, Eucken, Bergson, Poincaré, William James, Wundt, Nietzsche, Schiller, Lessing, Winkelman, Taine, Ruskin, Wilde, Menéndez Pelayo, Croce y Hegel. [4]

José Vasconcelos includes Bergson among the prominent thinkers who became the intellectual diet of his group:

> Paulatinamente vuelve a ganar terreno la metafísica; la *Crítica de la razón pura* se hizo el libro del día, y poco a poco aumentaron los lectores de Eucken y Boutroux, de Bergson, Poincaré, William James y Wundt. [5]

Earlier we cited an article in which Pedro Henríquez Ureña points out the "Ateneo's" indebtedness to Bergson and other contemporary philosophers. [6] In a letter to Alfonso Reyes he reaffirms this point:

---

[4] Juan Hernández Luna, ed., *Conferencias del Ateneo de la Juventud* (Mexico: Universidad Nacional Autónoma de México, 1962), p. 10.

[5] José Vasconcelos, "El movimiento intelectual contemporáneo de México," in *Conferencias del Ateneo de la Juventud,* p. 128.

[6] See Chapter I, p. 14.

D. Justo ya se refirió a las nuevas doctrinas filosóficas, que apenas habían comenzado a mencionarse en nuestras conferencias. En 1907 junto con el estudio de Grecia, surgió el estudio de la filosofía y la destrucción del positivismo. Gómez Robelo ya la hacía, basándose en Schopenhauer; Valenti, basándose en libros italianos; Caso y yo emprendimos la lectura de Bergson y de James y de Boutroux. De ahí data la renovación filosófica de México, que ahora es apoyada por otros. [7]

In our first chapter we stressed the importance of the "Ateneo de la Juventud" to the philosophical and aesthetic formation of the "Contemporaneos." This correspondence is clearly noted in the relationship between José Vasconcelos and Carlos Pellicer. Our poet, who served as secretary to Vasconcelos during his tenure as Minister of Public Instruction, is the chief spokesman of the Philosopher's theory of "americanismo tropical," and reflects, as we will demonstrate in the course of this chapter, Bergsonian philosophy directly or via the *Estética* of Vasconcelos. Let us begin by examining the themes which present a new view of reality and later some techniques which portray those same themes.

A. REALITY AS FLUX

Reality is not, according to Bergson, a fixed, static, measurable state existing externally and independently of the human mind. Reality cannot be objectified or divided into individual parcels to be studied and comprehended. Any attempt to divorce reality from its true essence, duration, is misrepresentation. The only manner by which we can hope to grasp the feeling of this reality is through intuitive perception. Vasconcelos agrees with the concept of reality as movement when he says:

> Todo cuanto concebimos como esencia, y salvo las formas del conocer, se presenta a nuestra conciencia en movimiento. Ello se debe a que cuanto percibimos es finito y es relativo. Y todo lo que es particular padece inquieto anhelo de integrarse a un devenir; todo nuestro ser con

---

[7] Pedro Henríquez Ureña, "Archivo de Alfonso Reyes," *Plural,* 10 (July, 1972), p. 22.

su ambiente está contenido así dentro de un ancho curso en cuyo seno hay remolinos de liberación. Y nada escapa definitivamente a su devenir mientras no se realiza lo Absoluto. Pues únicamente lo Absoluto tiene derecho a equilibrio estático. De allí que en el Universo sólo se concibe un ser inmóvil, el Ser Absoluto, y todo lo demás gira y decae, o se alza en espiral a fin de consumarse en la proximidad, la participación de lo Absoluto. [8]

There exist two distinct moments in Pellicer's poetry which reveal his adherence to the concept of reality as flux: one, his initial poems which speak not to a philosophical concept or a metaphysical view of reality, but express a natural and personal relationship the poet enjoys with reality; and two, he pursues the belief of reality as movement along a philosophical path, perhaps guided by Bergson and Vasconcelos, to a statement of a poetic based on this view of reality.

His initial poetic offering, *Colores en el mar,* is an expression of joy and bewilderment approximating a child's first contact with the beauty of Nature. Special emphasis is given to the sea. It is not, however, the romantic sea, symbol of the infinite mysteries and the transcendence of nature, but an impressionistic, jovial and musical phenomenon:

¡El Sol! ¡El Sol! ¡El Sol!...
Detrás de un arrebol
llegó aquel joven Sol.

Y el alba al encender
el gran faro del día
en la noche del Tiempo, todo lo desoía;
y yo volví a nacer.

Nubes en *sol* mayor
y olas en *la* menor.

La vida era tan bella como el amanecer.

Pareció que en el mar
se bañasen mil niños; así las olas eran
infantiles y claras de gritar.

[8] Vasconcelos, *Estética,* p. 173.

> Y una mujer pasaba
> toda dominical. (13)

This motif is repeated throughout the first book. Never do we see nature represented as a still life; it is alive, moving, singing, laughing, dancing, as in:

> Del sur llegó el andante del mar, vuelto
>   andantino.
> A lo lejos las olas acordadas se ven.
> Y al llegar a la playa, claras y
>   burbujeantes,
> abren escalas rápidas y brillantes. (14)

and:

> Pero como avanzara yo sobre el litoral,
> la ola arqueando ímpetus se retorció en
>   la arena
> dejando en mi lascivia tres algas por melena
> y un gran carcajada de espumas de cristal. (18)

The sea is not the only natural phenomenon represented as movement. In "La tempestad en los Andes" even mountains come to life:

> Lanzada la sierra sobre los paisajes
> tuerce y retuerce su fuerza total. (49)

And night is seen as an invader:

> Cuando la noche nos invadió
> bajábamos de los Andes (51)

Later in "Apuntes coloridos" a lake and the sky are represented as a movement of tones and colors:

> En una cuenca de los Andes
> rápidos y hostiles,
> se mueve un lago vibrante
> dueño de islotes y dulces confines.
>
> Muévense el verde y el azul
> hasta tonalizar nuevos colores,

> y en los blancos clarísimos de espuma
> hay difusión de flores.
>
> En el cielo hay una danza de nubes.
> El lago copia las mejores líneas
> y las robadas sombras blancas
> en la tarde se doran y se pintan.
> Se torna el lago mágica acuarela
> en las que formas toco y bebo tintas.   (54)

These poems, as we stated earlier, do not hint at a philosophical view of reality, but rather give a sense of the author's intimate contact with his poetic material. In a poem entitled "La danza" from *Hora y 20,* he shifts from a simple representation of reality as flux to a more precise image of a spiral movement:

> Movía el corazón ruedas doradas
> en un juego de sombras avivadas
> por la espiral que asciende y perfecciona,   (197)

Both Bergson and Vasconcelos [9] emphasized the particular character of movement in their views of reality. It is not a linear movement which can be divided into historic compartments, a movement with a fixed beginning and end, but a constant surging, pulsation, a circular movement best imagined as a spiral. "La danza" initiates the image of movement of reality as a spiral, an image which is repeated many times in the poetry which follows. In the poem, "Estudio y poema" (198-200) dedicated to José Vasconcelos he begins and ends with a view of reality as movement, "Las estrellas danzan" and the spiral image, "El Ganges sube en espiral alrededor del Himalaya." The fact that this poem, whose theme is the idea of reality as flux, is dedicated to Vasconcelos is no mere coincidence. In the initial poem of *Camino* he again utilizes the spiral image:

> Tus pasos fueron caminos
> de música. La danzó ·
> la espiral envuelta en hojas
>   de horas.
> Desnuda liberación.   (205)

---

[9] Vasconcelos, *Estética,* p. 173.

The movement of reality now becomes more than representation;
it reaches the force of a poetic. It is a quality he admires in the
poet Díaz Mirón who represents nature as an active, constantly
moving force. In "Oda a Díaz Míron" (212-216) Pellicer writes:

> ¡Alegría al idioma! Es tu fiesta,
> y los flácidos perros que te ladran
> ignoran al antílope en la siesta.
>
> Y desembarcó el mar junto a tu casa
> y es natural que agolpe tus poemas
> y un soplo litoral los dé en la plaza.
>
> Y hay agua viva en la boca de mayo,
> y una palmera se puso a bailar.
> Sesgó la tempestad su hermoso rayo
>
> y la lluvia encendió los naranjales,
> y el Sur bajo los puentes acrecía
> la copa de sus magnos festivales.   (215)

In "Esquemas para una oda tropical" it is again the spiral image
which is utilized to represent the life and movement of things:

> Entonces yo podría
> tolerar la epidermis
> de la vida espiral de la palmera,   (256)

and again in "Invitación al paisaje":

> Invitar al paisaje a que venga a mi mano,
> invitarlo a dudar de sí mismo,
> darle a beber el sueño del abismo
> en la mano espiral del cielo humano.   (285)

No more clearly does he utilize this image to present a Bergsonian
view of reality than in "Poema pródigo" where he writes:

> En mi casa de las nubes
> o bajo el cielo de los árboles,
> rodeado de todas las cosas creadas
> (oídas espirales del berbiquí mirada),   (301)

But the understanding and representation as flux is not without
problems as he points out in one of his sonnets from *Hora de junio*:

> Para mirar el cielo, qué trabajos
> ruedan los ojos turbios, siempre bajos.
> ¿Serán estrellas o huellas de estrellas?   (288)

Is it the thing we see or its shadow preserved by memory? This question is the essence of "Nocturno" which begins with the complaint:

> No tengo tiempo de mirar las cosas
> como yo lo deseo.
> Se me escurren sobre la mirada
> y todo lo que veo
> son esquinas profundas rotuladas con radio
> donde leo la ciudad para no perder tiempo.   (131)

Here the poet is a victim of the rapidity of modern life that prohibits him from seeing things as they really are and capsulizes the world into a "dato pequeño." He repeats his dissatisfaction with this manner of perceiving the reality of things:

> No tengo tiempo de mirar las cosas,
> casi las adivino.
> Una sabiduría ingénita y celosa
> me da miradas previas y repentinos trinos.
> Vivo en doradas márgenes; ignoro el central
>   gozo
> de las cosas.   (131)

He complains that he does not see things as they are, but as generalizations of previous experience ("Miradas previas"). Because of the rapidity of movement he is unable to experience the soul of things ("ignoro el central gozo/de las cosas"), and is obliged to understand them by their external trappings ("Vivo en doradas márgenes").

Thus we move from the concept of reality as flux, to the problem of perception and representation of this reality.

B.   PERCEPTION AND REPRESENTATION
OF REALITY AS FLUX

Both Bergson and Vasconcelos deal with the problem of perception of reality and come to the same general conclusions: that the intellect which deals in concepts is unable to grasp reality as duration; that concepts destroy the individuality of a thing by referring only to recognizable and general qualities possessed by the object; that ordinary perception is not equipped with the means to delve into the interior of things; and finally, that the power to lift the "thin veil" [10] which divides us from a true knowledge of things is a gift of the artist and the role of art.

Pellicer is aware of the problem of language that because of its communal nature tends to generalize and objectify reality. In the poem dedicated to Vasconcelos discussed above, he expresses the need to return to unnamed things:

> Fe de cosas sin nombre da su acento
> y el alma va como las melodías
> sobre las pausas ágiles del viento.
>
> Fe que dio al escalón perfectos pasos
> y enfrento la mirada a la áurea puerta
> por donde salen par albas y ocasos. (199)

In "Oda a Díaz Mirón" he expresses the frustration in having to use a language which is unable to express elemental nature:

> Aún se amargan los labios escolares
> de no saber decir como quisieran
> del fuego, de la tierra y de los mares. (212)

And in "Fragmentos" two brilliant metaphors reveal his dissatisfaction with words:

> ¡Las palabras!
> ¡Los tropeles pueriles
> sobre el espejo de la imagen!
>
> ¡Ah, las palabras,
> que llamaban a todas las cosas por su
>   apodo escolar!
> ¡Labios de las canciones que no volví a besar!
> (220)

---

[10] Henri Bergson, *Laughter,* trans. by Cloudesley Brereton and Fred Rothwell (New York: The Macmillan Co., 1928), p. 155.

The solution for Pellicer is to rid things of those external trappings which hide their true reality and make poetry the tool which converts a static and generalized view of reality into an intuition of duration, or as he states in "A la poesía," it is poetry as "Desnuda liberación." (205) Varieties of this image are repeated in "Concierto breve" where he begins:

> Con la voz descalza
> y el camino extranjero, sin preguntas,
> te ando y te desando,
> ciudad semilunar, aduana de la luna.   (243)

In "Esquemas para una oda tropical" he states:

> Yo quiero arder mis pies en los braseros
> de la angustia más sóla,
> para salir desnudo hacia el poema
> con las sandalias de aire que otros poros
> inocentes le den.   (256)

and in "El encuentro":

> Y en la muda sorpresa de mi sangre
> el espejo creador abrió su foco
> y salieron del baño las imágenes.   (250)

Besides his representation of the poetic image as cleansed and nude, it is noteworthy to mention his image of the poetic process as "espejo creador." It is not a mere reflection of reality, but a creative process as well. Thus it is not enough to merely represent or reflect flux, but it must be recreated in order that the reader may intuitively grasp its essence.

How then is the poet to communicate an intuition of reality as duration without succumbing to statement? Bergson provides the answer in his *Introduction to Metaphysics.* One cannot by language nor by imagery state an intuition of reality. But by surrounding the intuition with diverse images he may hope to evoke in the reader an intuition of the experience. [11] In Pellicer to under-

---

[11] Henri Bergson, *Selections from Bergson,* ed. Harold A. Larrabee (New York: Appleton-Century-Crofts, 1949), p. 9. Bergson writes: "many diverse images, borrowed from very different orders of things, may, by the conver-

stand it, or better yet, to feel it, one must abandon the intellect and concede to the power of the senses. As he suggests:

> Confesemos nuestra estupidez,
> alabemos nuestros sentidos:
> oíd, mirad, sentid.   (198)

His poetry is resplendent with examples of images that avoid statement, that depend on emotion and mood rather than literal interpretation. One cannot explain the reality of:

> Sabor de octubre en tus hombros,
> de abril tu mano da olor.
> Reflejo de cien espejos
>   tu cuerpo.
> Noche en las flautas mi voz.   (205)

It must be captured by the senses and experienced.

His "Poema elemental" is an attempt to express the elements not by statements, but through original and fresh images which can evoke the intuition of them from the reader. Thus air "es transparente/cual el silencio en una lectura prodigiosa." (207) By means of this metaphor he removes any generalized concept we might have of any one particular element by surrounding it and interpenetrating it with its opposite. The tensive relationship of the parts creates not a statement about the air (for the metaphor defies literal interpretation), but rather evokes tone, mood, in short, intuition of the experience. In like manner he says of water: "Aguas verticales, horizontal, cerámica y primera." (208) We must expect to experience things anew, as if it were our initial contact. As he says in the final poem of *Camino*:

---

gence of their action, direct consciousness to the precise point where there is a certain intuition to be seized. By choosing images as dissimilar as possible, we shall prevent any one of them from usurping the place of the intuition it is intended to call up since it would then be driven away at once by its rivals. By providing that in spite of their differences of aspect, they all require from the mind the same kind of attention, and in some sort the same degree of tension, we shall gradually accustom consciousness to a particular and clearly-defined disposition — that precisely which it must adopt in order to appear to itself as it really is, without any veil."

> Porque en mí se renuevan los sentidos
> como el aroma de una noche alzada
> a través de nostálgicos caminos. (250)

True to his word he invites us to see things with new eyes, to experience the joy of creating reality through fresh perception:

> Vámonos a la luna mongolfiera.
> Tres paisajes de yeso a nadie estorban
> a pesar de los tangos y palmeras.
>
> Y el que quiera
> se pintará con dramas las ojeras.
>
> Vámonos a las primeras
> orillas de la noche, con tijeras
> podadoras de estrellas y de espumas,
> las facilitadoras de las sumas
> del escalante precio de las fieras.
>
> El tigre adolescente
> pensativo en la arena se despinta.
> Se está borrando ya las tachaduras
> con que fue reprobada la lascivia
> del gasto de oro de sus carnes duras. (260)

This artistic perception is not a mirror of reality, it is, to use Pellicer's image, an "espejo creador." It orders the experience of duration of flux, and creates a reality unlike any other, the reality of the poem. We are in Pellicer's world, his play:

> Tengo a la ola de la mano y subo
> a mi país de imágenes do el piso
> es de espejo y caoba el cortinaje
> del teatro de la aurora.
>
> La función de esta noche en cuatro mares
> tendrá control. Las perlas de la entrada
> se echan al cuello de las más morenas.
> Puntualidad y esmero de sonidos. (261)

We cannot overemphasize the importance of this idea. There is no absolute reality, only duration. What we experience is the poet's reality as he orders and recreates flux into a sensual experience which evokes from us the intuition of duration. In "Grupas de nubes" the clouds represent a visual symbol of an everchanging reality which is inexpressible until the poet gives it a sensual character which the reader can experience:

> En los grupos de nubes,
> a inquietudes mi vida tornasola
> su afán de cambio y su ojo de ser cumbre,
> Su gran imperio en fuga
> organiza la tarde. Cuatro niños
> dejan en sed la fuente jardinera
> y se llevan el agua con sus tintas jugadas.
>
> En el cielo hay país con primavera.
>
> Su majestad con corona de vidrio
> espera en las colinas la llegada
> de volcán y volcana
> en viaje ópalo. Hay a través del aire hilos
> que arrenglonan la zona disponible
> de lo decir poético.
> Y al poste divisor del trompo aéreo
> ato las aventuras instantáneas
> del vivir en cambiar, cielo deseo.   (269)

The poet here is not a prisoner of reality, but demonstrates his mastery and superiority. Reality exists only because of his poem; not prior to its creation, but because of the act of creation. As he states in a later poem, reality is only a group of figures until it is given shape and meaning by poetry:

> Los grupos de figuras
> equilibro con onzas de poema
> —la voz lineal y las palabras mudas.   (272)

Three poems which appear in succession in *Hora de junio* reveal the supremacy of the reality of the poem: "Poética del paisaje," "Retórica del paisaje," and "Invitación al paisaje." In the first we see the reality of things as deriving their existence from the elements of poetry:

> Pasa la nube a tono
> con la punta del lápiz quebradiza.
> Y está la pausa en trono.

(Tiempo y color: yo les doy un abono
y designo banquera a una sonrisa ...)

Una paloma negra
entablera su vuelo y otras cuatro
buscan la aguja mágica del cuento.
Mientras vira la nube yo me ausento
a revisar las cuentas de mi teatro.

El patio lo ocupó el endecasílabo;
el palco y la platea
ciertos traje-de-cola alejandrinos.
En galería
hay uno que otro gratis sin oficio. (281)

In the second poem he says clearly and unequivocally:

Porque la realidad es cosa mía,
es decir, lo que usted nunca verá,
en un plato le da Santa Lucía
los ojos convenientes. (282)

An example of this reality follows:

la flora es intocable; en cutis verde
la aguja del tatuaje, defensiva
punza el tacto a distancia.
Chillan flores carnales
sobre el nopal que sesga sus etapas
rimadas en elipse. Si hundo los pedales
surge en esbelto prisma el cactus órgano,
cuyo bisel alfiletero agarra
pequeñas nubes de heno.
El castus cuya fálica erección
límite varonil marca al terrano. (282)

Later in the poem he reveals the true nature of his art:

Si echo la cara atrás de lo que digo,
la cordillera sube hasta las nieves
perpetuas. (283)

Notice he uses a form of the verb "decir" rather than a form of
"ver" to refer to his reality. The reality of his poems exists because
he says it, expresses it, and not because he sees it. Therein lies the

all important distinction. It is not an art that is created from a vision of reality on which it is dependent for veracity, but rather an art which creates a reality, unique and independent.

Due to its importance and crystalization of all we have just discussed relative to the theme of poetic reality we will transcribe the third poem, "Invitación al paisaje" in its entirety:

Invitar al paisaje a que venga a mi mano,
invitarlo a dudar de sí mismo,
darle a beber el sueño del abismo
en la mano espiral del cielo humano.

Que al soltar los amarres de los ríos
la montaña a sus mármoles apele
y en la cumbre el suspiro que se hiele
tenga el valor frutal de dos estíos.

Convencer a la nube
del riesgo de la altura y de la aurora,
que no es el agua baja la que sube
sino la plenitud de cada hora.

Atraer a la sombra
al seno de rosales jardineros.
(Suma el amor la resta de lo que amor se nombra
y da a comer la sobra a un palomar de ceros.)

¡Si el mar quisiera abandonar sus perlas
y salir de la concha . . . !
Si por no derramarlas o beberlas
—copa y copo de espumas— las olvida.

Quién sabe si la piedra
que en cualquier recodo es maravilla
quiera participar de exacta exedra,
taza-fuente-jardín-amor-orilla.

Y si aquel buen camino
que va, viene y está, se inutiliza
por el inexplicable desatino
de una cascada que lo magnetiza.

¿Podrán venir los árboles con toda
su escuela abecedaria de gorjeos?
(Siento que se aglomeran mis deseos
como el pueblo a las puertas de una boda.)

El río allá es un niño y aquí un hombre
que negras hojas junta en un remanso.
Todo el mundo le llama por su nombre
y le pasa la mano como a un perro manso.

¿En qué estación han de querer mis huéspedes
descender? ¿En otoño o primavera?
¿O esperarán que el tono de los céspedes
sea el ángel que anuncie la manzana primera?

De todas las ventanas, que una sola
sea fiel y se abra sin que nadie la abra.
Que se deja cortar como amapola
entre tantas espigas, la palabra.

Y cuando los invitados
ya estén aquí —en mí—, la cortesía
única y sóla por los cuatro lados,
será dejarlos sólos, y en signo de alegría
enseñar los diez dedos que no fueron tocados
sino
por
la
sola
poesía.   (285 & 286)

No one poem in *Material poético* gives a clearer statement of Pellicer's poetic and vision of reality. Poetry for him is to break away from a static, conceptualized, and generalized view of reality. It is a creation of reality that is pure and untouched except by the poem in which it exists.

Before we end our discussion of perception and its role in the creation of a poetic reality, let us return to a discussion of its function. Of particular interest to us now is the role of memory in the act of perception.

C. MEMORY AND PERCEPTION

Pellicer raises the question of the participation of memory in the act of perception when he looks at the sky and asks: "¿Serán estrellas o huellas de estrellas?" (288) Memory and perception in their pure states are independent of one another, but in man function in complementary interaction. For man is, as is all reality, duration. His present state is a constant spiral that blends past and present as it moves into the future. His perception of an object or phenomenon is interpenetrated with previous experiences of like objects or phenomena and make of perception a highly personal and creative act. Since we have accepted the idea that reality is a flux which is ordered and made sensual by the perception of the past, it is only one more step to explore the degree to which memory affects the act of perception.

In *Matter and Memory* Bergson emphasizes that the acts of perception and memory are simultaneous:

> with the immediate and present data of our senses we mingle a thousand details out of our past experience. In most cases these memories supplant our actual perceptions, of which we then retain only a few hints, thus using them merely as 'signs' that recall to us former images. [12]

The role of memory in the perception of present sense data was the subject of many late nineteenth and early twentieth century writers (Marcel Proust, Virginia Woolf, James Joyce to mention a few). William James who was the first to use the term "stream of consciousness" to describe Bergson's durational flux [13] also termed the interpenetration of memory and perception of present sense data as "the specious present" which he defined as "a bow and a stern, as it were — a rearward — and a forward looking end." [14]

Most frequent evidence of the mixture of memory with present perception is found in Pellicer's poems dealing with the absence of a lover. In these poems the memory of the lover impregnates and modifies the landscape of the poem. In "La noche" he writes:

> Bajo la dulce penumbra
> de la noche de luna de la ausencia,
> canta el poeta su tristeza.
> ... ...
> Esta noche la música del cielo
> juega en astros nuevos íntimas escalas.

---

[12] Bergson, *Selections,* p. 24.

[13] Shiv K. Kumar, *Bergson and the Stream of Consciousness Novel* (New York: New York University Press, 1963), p. 13.

[14] Kumar, p. 15.

> El aire está peinado por tus manos
> lejanas,
> como un vuelo
> de garzas. (104)

This theme is repeated again in "El recuerdo":

> Tu ausencia ha dejado sobre las piedras
> una florecita que tal vez es negra.
> Y en la vida
> de la piedra y la flor tras de tu sombra,
> mis manos ven y oyen y graban un signo
> que compendia todas las cosas.
> En las horas,
> en que se perpetúan los instantes
> de tu ausencia presente de paloma. (161)

In his poems of travel the new and strange landscapes reflect the constant presence of the lover:

> Corono tu recuerdo desde una isla griega
> que vidria el sol y el tiempo no pasa
>   sino juega.
> Al cielo de tus ojos no volveré. Por ti,

> vino de Chipre bebo, sombras de vino entono,
> y en el baile de luces tu recuerdo corono
> con las mismas palabras que en tus ojos
>   bebí. (175)

In "Nocturno de Constantinopla" the objects of an exotic landscape lose their particular significance and are transformed by the continuous presence of memory:

> Los nombres se olvidan poco a poco
> bajo la estrella reinante del
> collar de tu recuerdo.
> Y sueño en tus ojos
> las aventuras inefables, tus sutiles besos,
> entre la bruma de oro
> de la historia semitonada
> en nuestro amor perfecto. (177)

It is not a passive memory which collects past images, but one that transforms the perceptive reality into a personal and interior vision:

> Y la dicha de haberte amado tanto
> me transforma en un dios ordenador de sueños.
> Tuyas son estas cosas que salen de mis ojos
> para permanecer. (177)

In a somewhat lighter vein the force of memory plays upon him when he views the sun in Paris and says:

> Acércate, no te voy a hacer nada.
> Te atemoriza mi voz de agua nueva y el ruido
> de mis pies sobre las casas.
> Mira el retrato de tus hermanos de América,
> populares como los toreros y los pelotaris,
> ágiles y jóvenes. (194)

The Parisian sun is pale in contrast to the vivid memories he has of the sun in this native tropics. The Parisian sun is "Sol bibliotecario y sacristán," (194) and later, "sol de chimenea" (195). The creative force of memory is obvious in "Pausa Naval" where the images of the sea evoked by memory recreate an urban landscape in brilliant and daring metaphors:

> Al bajar del tranvía,
> pisé la estrella naútica y el timo
> del pie herido de océanos,
> halló la pausa hidráulica deseada
> y echó a huir en la voz su tren de voces
> vía-libre, vía-libre, vía-libre.
> ... ...
> El mar que parte plaza en las arenas,
> el mar a fuego de la China en lujo.
> Doña Isabel vendiendo los tamales
> de joyas,
> y las navegaciones del escándalo
> soltadas como esbeltos arrecifes
> de alquiler hacia el préstamo de América.
> Bajaron las palmeras
> de las trescientas olas automóviles
> y se bañaron de aire de colinas
> al rótulo naval Río de Janeiro. (262)
> ... ...
> Pausa naval al bajar del tranvía.
> A cuatrocientos kilómetros del mar
> escribo.
> Gracias por la risa y la sonrisa y las marinas
> que al asfalto nocturno me vienes a dejar. (264)

In Pellicer the mixture of images evoked by memory with sense data received by immediate perception creates a totally new reality, unlike any that could exist outside of the poem. Ultimately it leads to the destruction of traditional temporal boundaries of the past, present and future and creates a "specious present" or a state described by Bergson as "the invisible progress of the past gnawing into the future." [15] Let us now examine this concept of time and its representation in the poetry of Pellicer.

D. TIME

Given the idea of reality as durational flux, a constant becoming which is reality itself, and the role of memory in the act of perception, one can easily understand that time in this context is unlike the traditional, utilitarian concept it has acquired in Western civilization. Time as duration is incapable of being measured. Years, months, days, etc. are only spatialized concepts which break up time in utilitarian and pragmatic units. Time, in Bergsonian terms, is elastic, a constantly moving and growing state which contains past, present and future as interpenetrated and indivisible states.

A Bergsonian concept of time was for Pellicer not a radical stance, but an attitude which was inherent in his Mexican background. Pellicer's emotional and academic attachment to his precolumbian heritage is well known, thus it is logical to assume that his acceptance of a temporal attitude unlike that of Western man had its natural roots in his past and was buoyed by the revelations of Bergson and Vasconcelos. As Octavio Paz reveals, "time was not an empty, abstract measurement to the Aztecs, but rather something concrete, a force or substance or fluid perpetually being used up." [16] The parallel of the precolumbian cyclical concept of time to Bergson's *durée réelle* is obvious.

A cyclical concept of time is introduced early in *Pellicer's* work in "Uxmal," a poem from *Piedra de sacrificios.* Here he speaks of the glorious Indian past as manifest in this ancient Mayan city. The

---

[15] Bergson, *Selections,* p. 56.
[16] Octavio Paz, *The Labyrinth of Solitude* (New York: Grove Press, 1961), p. 93.

first part of the poem is written exclusively in the preterite tense. But suddenly there is a shift to a mixture of present, future, and past:

> Uxmal,
> llena de ingenieros poéticos,
> opulenta y sepulcral.
> Danzarán tus serpientes endiosadas
> sobre las piedras verdes y sonoras
> cuando las horas de luces plateadas
> hilan estrellas y elevan auroras.
> Uxmal,
> tus escalinatas las he recorrido
> y en tus panoramas he puesto mis manos.
> Uxmal,
> tú llenaste mi corazón,
> y de tu raza culta es mi alegría
> y mi vaso sincero de pasión.
> Tú tocaste la puerta de mi corazón,
> Uxmal;
> se alza una voz,
> se oye otra voz.
> Uxmal,
> es tu divina sensación. (66 & 67)

Thus Pellicer informs the reader that Uxmal, a city belonging to a past civilization, is vibrantly alive, and will continue to live in the future.

A similar treatment is offered Cuauhtémoc, last of the Aztec rulers, in the poem which closes *Piedra*.... In the first two parts which recall the tragic history of the young Aztec monarch the use of the past tense predominates. The last part of the poem draws the past into the present:

> Y ahora mismo todavía
> lo miro, lo palpo y lo siento   (97)

as Cuauhtémoc moves on a cyclical temporal path to again become a vital force in the present and future:

> ¡Oh Señor! ¡Oh gran Rey! ¡Tlacatecutli!
> ¡Oh solemne y trágico jefe de hombres!
> ¡Oh dulce y feroz Cuauhtémoc!
> ¡Tu vida es la flecha más alta que ha herido

> los ojos del Sol y ha seguido volando en el
>   cielo!
> Pero en el cráter de mi corazón
> hierve la fe que salvará a tus pueblos.   (97)

A representation of time as substance rather than an abstract measurement is presented in "Estudios" from *Hora y veinte*:

> Las horas se adelgazan;
> de una salen diez.
> Es el trópico,
> prodigioso y funesto.
> Nadie sabe qué hora es.   (191)

This is not time in the sense of a mechanized, commercial world, run on schedules and deadlines, but time in the tropics where "Las noticias van a tener tiempo/de cambiar de camisa" (191). Time here is elastic, fluid and immeasurable:

> Y en una línea nueva de la garza,
> renace el tiempo,
> lento, fecundo, ocioso,
> creado para soñar y ser perfecto.   (193)

Note that he says "renace el tiempo" and not "pasa el tiempo." Time is seen here as a rebirth, a constant becoming and not as a linear trajectory toward the future.

As the poetry progresses we see a movement from a natural expression of sympathy for a circular concept of time, to a more sophisticated attempt to articulate a metaphysical concept of time along Bergsonian lines as in the metaphor:

> Y estoy en ti.
> Casi como en mí dentro de pocos años.
> ¡Y pasa un minuto y ya siento
> los recuerdos del porvenir!   (243)

And in "Esquemas para una oda tropical" he writes:

> Las brisas limoneras
> ruedan en el remanso de los ríos
> Y la iguana nostálgica de siglos
> en los perfiles largos de su tiempo
> fue, es, y será.   (258)

Pellicer in his earlier poetry complains of time in the modern world which enslaves man and prohibits him from perceiving the world of things around him, "No tengo tiempo de mirar las cosas/como yo lo deseo" (131). But he later understands time not as an abstract master of his will, but as a substance that is durational flux. It is a reality over which he gains supreme control; "La tarde en automóvil detuve sobre el puente" (272). He stops the movement of time and enters it and beholds a reality that would be invisible to normal vision:

> En el piso cincuenta
> las viguetas de fierro, paralelas,
> vida cuadrangular dan al espacio.
> Dos obreros azules
> remachan un amarre. Los martillos
> enloquecen los átomos de fierro
> y hacen brillar el hongo del tornillo.   (274)

Now that we have examined some aspects of durational flux in the poetry of Pellicer, let us look at some of the devices used to portray duration in poetry.

E.   Poetic Devices of Duration

Although there are a number of studies concerning the Bergsonian aesthetic and its relationship to modern prose, in particular the "stream of consciousness" novel, there are very few dealing with its application to modern poetry (we are excluding studies on surrealism, automatic writing, etc.).

In the aforementioned study of Bergson and the "stream of consciousness" novel, several devices to portray durational flux are discussed. Included among these are prepositional participles, parentheses, coordinative conjunctions, the imperfect tense and dots. We will discuss some of these as they relate to Pellicer's poetry in addition to some that are uniquely applicable to poetry.

1.   Parentheses and Dash

Of the devices to be discussed in this section, the use of the parentheses and the dash appear with the greatest frequency. The first two books of his poems make limited use of these devices, but beginning with *6, 7 poemas* and continuing through *Hora de junio* they enter into his poetry as a major recourse to portray aspects of durational flux.

His early poems employ the parentheses as a poetical aside which lends a casual and often times a conversational tone to the poem:

> Yo por idiosincrasia (¡conocida!)   (20)

and:

> Fue ésa la noche más negra
> que nunca hubo caído sobre los Andes.
> (El mundo debió haber sufrido
> los más lúgubres trances.)   (51)

and:

> Yo sé (aunque no lo digas), que somos
>   predilectos...   (94)

Or they give an additional descriptive effect as in:

> Más una tarde aguas fuertes costosísimas
> húbela de abandonar.
> (Crepúsculo desde el puente de Brooklyn
> y última hoja otoñal.)   (75)

In his later poems the dash and the parentheses portray the act of perception and the writing of poetry not as ordered and progressive, but as a series of unrelated and at times contrary images that arise simultaneously:

> Porque las bestias y los ángeles,
> (amor ama al que ama),
> enfriarán el rayo en las piscinas.   (117)

The poetic aside written in parentheses removes the feeling of an accomplished work belonging to the past and creates a sense of immediacy:

> (¡Oh amigos míos,
> siento que el lápiz escribe solo

estas antiguas palabras!)   (124)
... ...
Al año de morir todos los días
los frutos de mi voz dijeron tanto
y tan calladamente, que unos días

vivieron a la sombra de aquel canto.
(Aquí la voz se quiebra y el espanto
de tanta soledad llena los días.)   (268)

and finally:

Y lejos, unas lomas
de un verde "golf" y bosque a la derecha
y un tajo en carne viva su desnivel aploma.
(Un ocho de palomas
divide mi atención en varias fechas.)   (280)

In "Variaciones sobre un tema de viaje" his description of Jerusalem and meditations on the sacrifice of Christ evoke memories of yet another who dedicated his whole life to a cause. The memory evoked by perception is set aside in parentheses and has the character of a poem within a poem, the simultaneous appearance of present and past:

Dichosa piedra que sentiste un día
su pie ya grueso, su profunda mano
o su silencio y su melancolía.

(Sobre la siesta tropical temblaba
mi adolescencia ante la dulce quinta
en que nubló Bolívar sus postreras mañanas.

Y maduré en el alma submarina
la perla viva que en su iris llora
su más noble temblor de sangre herida.

Sangre augusta, la heroica
sangre del héroe disputan soles
brotados de palmeras a caobas.

Pero del sitio heroico al sitio santo
las palabras caminan silenciosas
con temblor de universos en las manos.)

> Jerusalén de luna pavorosa
> me invadía esas noches que rodaron
> a mí como altos trenes sobre pequeñas cosas.   (153)

In the midst of a poem singing the achievements of Bolívar, nature is suddenly infused with the grandeur of the hero:

> Tus funerales siguen en marcha
> entre el mar y los Andes, junto al agua y
>   junto al cielo
> (La Aurora sale del mar
> con un trágico gesto
> y la Noche engrandece su severidad noble
> en la solidez monumental de los cedros.)   (171)

By the use of the parentheses the poet allows us to experience the material of his poem as he did. The parentheses avoid the need for logical progression and clarity. Comments to the reader, to himself, seemingly unrelated images, all coexist simultaneously in the creative act. In "estrofas del mar marino" we hear the poet coaxing the words forward to the poem:

> (¡Vámonos, palabra, vámonos
> del alma que ésta diciendo
> sus ocho sílabas tristes,
> ochenta, ochocientas... Vámonos!)   (290)

The dash serves the same purposes as does the parentheses, and, in addition, permits the poet to create images evoked by the perception of some sense data:

> Los grupos de palomas
> —notas, claves, silencios, alteraciones—,
> modifican lugares de la loma.   (163)
> ... ...
> Fuiste en mi vida el vuelo de más largo
>   horizonte.
> Se queman en mi vida tus ojos solitarios.
> Nuestras dos soledades —música de la noche—
> ligan a las estrellas los inefables actos.   (221)
> ... ...
> Y tu hallazgo —creación de un planeta—.   (233)

2. *Polysyndeton*

No one device captures the pulsation, and rhythmical movement of durational flux more dramatically than the polysyndeton, the repetitive use of the conjunction "y". Numerous examples of this device exist in Pellicer's poetry:

> Y allí nos encontramos
> los hindúes, los javaneses, los mayas,
> y conversamos de nuestros pájaros,
> de nuestros árboles
> y de las historias sagradas
> y de las ciudades que se suicidan
> y de las montañas
> desde donde se ve el mundo.   (190)
> ... ...
> Y desembarco el mar junto a tu casa
> y es natural que agolpe tus poemas
> y un soplo litoral los de en la plaza.
>
> Y hay agua viva en la boca de mayo,
> y una palmera se puso a bailar.
> Sesgo la tempestad su hermoso rayo
>
> y la lluvia encendió los naranjales,
> y el Sur bajo los puentes acrecía
> la copa de sus magnos festivales.   (215)
> ... ...
> Las palabras vagabundas
> en la mala suerte de mi sonrisa.
> Y el sueño resucitado en plena tarde
> junto a las maquinarias y las ruinas.
> Y hablarte con la voz con que hablo al viento
> y a la sombra.
> Y la voz que me dice: "Perdone, pero está
>   usted en la calle."
> Y encontrarme casi desnudo.   (220)

The most common use of the polysyndeton is at the beginning of each verse. In "El encuentro" Pellicer employs it in the interior as well:

> Y tu mirada tersa me encamina
> hacia el estanque intacto, y se coagula
> mi sombra en él como la lluvia alpina.

Y así se modeló lo que modula
entre pausas de fónicos mensajes
la ola eterna que el espacio anula.

Y sentí que crecían los paisajes
imprevistos. Y el agua de la onda
subía de raíces a ramajes.   (248 & 249)

The repetitiveness and its rhythmical spacing create both the sound
and feeling of a movement which is surging, growing — a sense of
continuous becoming.

In addition to the polysyndeton using "y" Pellicer employs the
preposition "a" for the same purpose in "Esquemas para una oda
tropical":

La oda tropical a cuatro voces
podrá llegar, palabra por palabra,
a beber en mis labios,
a amarrarse en mis brazos,
a golpear en mi pecho,
a sentarse en mis piernas,
a darme la salud hasta matarme
y a esparcirme en sí misma,
a que yo sea a vuelta de palabras,
palmera y antílope,
ceiba y caimán, helecho y ave-lira,
tarántula y orquídea, zenzontle y anaconda.   (259)

A further modification appears in "Dúos marinos" where the first
four verses begin with the words "el mar":

El mar diurno en la sombra de sus naves.
El mar nocturno en el farol de proa.
El mar del día que voltea el día.
El mar de noche que el timón platea.   (265)

3. *Enjambment*

Another frequently employed device to portray the flow of
reality is the use of enjambment or the continuous movement from
one stanza to the next as in:

Doré ritmos que a veces suelo olvidar. Y
echado

sobre los dulces tréboles al pie del Partenón,
pongo a danzar los lápices. Y el verso nace
    atado

a una columna rota y a un gran muro labrado.
Porque a un noble temblor la luz ha desbordado
la mano silenciosa que rige el corazón. (173)

and :

Un paso en el camino. El horizonte eleva
el gigantesco globo del cielo. Se abre y lleva
la mano una caricia panorámica y pura

por Curazao. Nacen suspiros holandeses.
Y ojo que vio, se torna tono que en telas dura
para esperar sin tedio los barcos y los
    meses.   183)

This device, when used to divide a metaphor between two
stanzas, creates even a more powerful sensation of durational flux :

Y fue que de Marsella —labios, viajes—,
partí sin almanaque o compromiso
llevándome de sesgo algún celaje

del último pañuelo
conque a todo color alguien pusiera
corbatas a los muelles del olvido. (147)
... ...
Día de dichas póstumas, día previsto.
Y tu presencia en filtro de tiempos y de cartas,
y mi fe empobrecida de no volver a verte
y tú siempre en mis ojos, en mi oído, en mis
    altas
cadenas de silencio cuyo eslabón cerré
para arrastrar a veces entre la noche un ruido
que disperse los síntomas de no volverte a
    ver. (182)

Here the nature of the poem demands a continuous reading from
stanza to stanza, for a pause would destroy not only the sense of
flow, but also the effectiveness of the metaphors.

4. Chaotic enumeration

The inclusion of chaotic enumeration under the category of devices used to portray reality as durational flux could be criticized, since its development is independent of that particular philosophy. We will demonstrate, however, that in Pellicer's poetry it becomes one of his most effective means of understanding modern reality as durational flux.

Leo Spitzer, in his study of chaotic enumeration in modern poetry, points out that enumeration itself is not a modern poetical device, but in past literature appeared under names such as "anáfora" and "asíndeton." [17] The modern usage of the device, contends Spitzer, has its origins in the poetry of Walt Whitman:

> Parece, en efecto, que es a Whitman a quien debemos estos catálogos del mundo moderno, deshecho en una polvareda de cosas heterogéneas, que se integran no obstante en su visión grandiosa y majestuosa del Todo-Uno. [18]

Chaotic enumeration is characterized by the naming and grouping of disparate and seemingly unrelated things: the exotic with the familar, the gigantic with the minuscule, products of nature with products of man, etc. [19]

Saul Yurkievich reveals that chaotic enumeration can be either "conjunctive," as in Whitman, or "disjunctive," as in Rimbaud who enumerates things "en mera coexistencia, sin amalgamarlos, como fragmentos superpuestos de una realidad desarticulada y desordenada." [20]

We can observe "conjunctive" chaotic enumeration in Pellicer's poems which deal with America as a unified whole, both in a

---

[17] Leo Spitzer, *La enumeración caótica en la poesía moderna* (Buenos Aires: Universidad de Buenos Aires, 1945), p. 25. See also: Leo Spitzer, "El conceptismo interior de Pedro Salinas," *Revista Hispánica Moderna* VII (1941), p. 40, and Detlev W. Schumann, "Enumerative Style and its Significance in Whitman, Rilke, Werfel," *Modern Language Quarterly* (June, 1942), pp. 171-204.

[18] Spitzer, p. 25.

[19] Spitzer, p. 26.

[20] Saúl Yurkievich, *Modernidad de Apollinaire* (Buenos Aires: Editorial Losada, 1968), p. 251.

historical, as well as geographical sense. In the "Oda" which initiates
Piedra... he enumerates:

> Y sobre el Golfo de México y el Mar Caribe;
> sobre el Mar Atlántico y el Mar Pacífico;
> sobre el Popocatépetl y el Momotombo,
> el Chimborazo y el Sorata;
> sobre el Usumacinta y el Orinoco
> y el Amazonas y el Plata,
> la Cruz del Sur abre su cuerpo armonioso.   (63)

and:

> Cuauhtémoc, joven y heroico,
> Atahualpa y Caupolicán.
> Bolívar y San Martín,
> y Pedro emperador del Brasil
> y Sucre y Morelos y Juárez
> y Artigas y Morazán y José Martí.   (64)

In "Scherzo" we see again "conjunctive" enumeration to express
those elements which are pleasing to him, not in any logical progression or related association, but as they happen to come to his
mind at the time of writing the poem:

> Y el mar dorado
> que coloridas olas serpentea
> bajo los vinos suaves de la aurora.
> Y en la arena de oro
> la huella viva de los pies desnudos.
> Y en el cuerpo desnudo y contundente
> la primera salpicadura del baño.
> Y las nubes llenas de semejanzas
> familiares.
> Y la alegría sin esperanza
> destas horas sin pares.   (121)

The only authentic use of "disjunctive" enumeration appears in the
poem "Divulgación del puerto":

> Momento inexorable de ignorancia,
> estupidez y miseria.
> El íntimo desorden de mi raza.
> Kant aplastado por Inglaterra.
> La inutilidad de mi vida.

> El mendigo que espera.
> La Navidad estéril de la obrerita.
> Los ricos y la ingratitud eterna.
> Y sobre todas las cosas,
> la infinita tristeza
> de Nuestro Señor Jesucristo,
> en las últimas tardes de Galilea. (75)

Here is a vision of a fragmented and confusing reality which the poet can only express in this alogical and chaotic array of images. Enumeration functions here as a device to express the chaos of modern existence as opposed to drawing any significance or relevance to its various manifestations.

In many of his poems chaotic enumeration functions as a device similar to stream of consciousness, to portray the act of perception as it is affected by memory in the creation of images. In "Elegía" he presents a series of unrelated images which are brought forth by a feeling of melancholy:

> Desde el balcón, se ve:
> han pasado muchos automóviles.
> Desde el balcón, se piensa:
> odio todos los libros.
> Estoy triste porque no soy bueno,
> Domingo. Uno desos estúpidos
> domingos sin sol.
> La catedral parece que está hipotecada.
> Yo me muero de ganas
> de huir
> de mí.
> Parece que he comido manzanas
> yanquis. (119)

In another poem entitled "Elegía" he enumerates a series of images evoked by the aroma of the sea:

> El sabor del mar,
> el sabor del mar.
>
> Archipiélagos, ladrones, paisajes mágicos.
> La vuelta al odio. El canto del amor.
> La ciudad telefónica, el precio romántico.
>
> Y tu hallazgo —creación de un planeta—, (233)

And in *Exágonos* we find an entire poem composed in a chaotic array of images:

> En el mar no hay invierno ni otoño
> y las mujeres cumplen siempre cuarenta años.
> Los poetas fracasan un poco
> y Ulises no fue más que un pobre diablo.
> Futuros recuerdos. Languidez. Nocturnos.
> En una nube viene la Virgen con dos santos.   (318)

Chaotic enumeration in Pellicer, while adhering in large part to the explanations of this device discussed earlier, is yet one more representation of reality as durational flux. This device presents reality, not as an orderly mass moving in a chronological order, but as a constantly expanding, spiraling movement. It presents a reality in which past, present and future coexist and intermingle. A reality which Pellicer captures in the image "Futuros recuerdos."

VI

STYLISTIC EXPRESSION OF REALITY:
THE METAPHOR

There is a marked tendency in critical studies on the poetry of Pellicer to avoid any substantive discussion of his metaphorical expression. [1] Most have been satisfied in dealing with content as if it were something distinct from form. Pellicer's imagery, as modern imagery in general, has evoked terms such as "difficult," "obscure," "private," etc. We will admit to the difficulty and, to a certain extent, its personal character, but reject the tag of obscurity. One of the objectives of this chapter is to demonstrate that Pellicer's imagery is far from obscure. His metaphors illuminate and express a poetic reality beyond the limits of normal perception. They are truer in their expression than the transparent metaphors based on abstract concepts of an exterior objective reality which lend themselves to facile and immediate interpretation.

We recognize that Pellicer's metaphorical usage does not originate with him. It represents a stage in the often times dialectical progress of metaphorical doctrine. In order to fully comprehend the significance of Pellicer's contribution to this aspect of poetry, it is essential to view it from a historical perspective. Thus prior to actual discussion of metaphor in Pellicer's poetry, we will present a brief, and admittedly eclectic, history of the development of modern metaphorical doctrine.

The reader will notice in the discussion to follow a somewhat fluid movement between the terms "image," "imagery," and met-

---

[1] Exceptions to this statement are the studies of Dauster, Paz, Ponce de Hurtado and Roggiano. See bibliography.

aphor." By image we mean a verbal expression capable of arousing sensual or emotional responses in the reader. Under the general category image we will find specific tropes which are distinguished by function or execution: simile, comparison, synesthesia, metonymy, synecdoche and metaphor, among others. In metaphor the distinguishing characteristics are that of transference — meaning of one term to that of another, or the interaction of the two terms.

Until the mid-nineteenth century metaphorical doctrine gravitated around two doctrines which had their beginnings in Aristotle. [2] The first, and most limiting, is called the doctrine of ornament and relegates metaphorical expression to the role of elevating language to ornate and dignified expression. The second, the doctrine of analogy, while expanding the possibilities of the metaphor to an interaction of two terms, was still required to respond to such *a priori* considerations as appropriateness, validity and truth.

While the romantics had rebelled against neo-classic restrictions in poetry, they were unable to wrestle the metaphor from its Aristotelian confines. As C. M. Bowra points out: "Despite their revolt against the eighteenth century, the Romantics had not completely abandoned its habit of abstract expression." [3] They had not yet removed the metaphor from its dependency on an exterior reality and a concept of poetic appropriateness and truth. In other words, they tried to make the poem *mean* something through abstract expression, rather than saying it through original and fresh imagery. The continuation of this aspect of the revolt was to be spearheaded by twentieth century poets and critics.

A. MODERN INTERPRETATION OF THE
DOCTRINE OF ANALOGY

Where the Doctrine of Ornament was to find many adverse critics in the modern epoch, the Doctrine of Analogy was better suited to express the nature and function of the metaphor. Among

---

[2] The exception to this generalization is the achievements of the baroque and metaphysical poets. See various studies in *The Metaphysical Poets,* ed. Frank Kermode (New York: Fawcett World Library, 1969). Also Dámaso Alonso, *Estudios y ensayos gongorinos* (Madrid: Gredos, 1955).

[3] C. M. Bowra, *The Romantic Imagination* (Cambridge, Massachusetts: Harvard University Press, 1949), p. 276.

the chief supporters of this view of metaphor was J. Middleton Murray who wrote:

> All metaphor and simile can be described as the analogy by which the human mind explores the universe of quality and charts the non-measurable world. [4]

In *The Problem of Style* he adds:

> Try to be precise and you are bound to be metaphorical; you simply cannot help establishing affinities between all the provinces of the animate and inanimate world... [5]

C. Day-Lewis views the metaphor not simply as finding similitude between two objects, but in uncovering the "relationship" of the objects:

> ...every image recreates not merely an object but an object in the context of an experience, and thus an object as part of a relationship. Relationship being in the very nature of metaphor, if we believe that the universe is a body wherein all men and all things are "members of one another," we must allow metaphor to give a "partial intuition of the whole world." [6]

Here one recognizes the metaphor's function as the act of uncovering the hitherto unseen. It is not an act of creating the relationship, but rather discovering its existence in the universal body of all things.

It was the analogical function of the metaphor which served to formulate I. A. Richards' now famous terminology for the different parts of the metaphor. In the *Philosophy of Rhetoric* he uses the term "tenor" to express the figure which possesses the meaning, and "vehicle" for the conveyor of this meaning. [7] Thus it is the "tenor" interacting with the "vehicle" which uncovers the analog-

---

[4] J. Middleton Murray, "Metaphor," in *Shakespeare Criticism 1919-35,* ed. Bradby (New York: Oxford University Press, 1936), p. 234.

[5] J. Middleton Murray, *The Problem of Style* (London-New York: Oxford University Press, 1922), p. 83.

[6] C. Day-Lewis, *The Poetic Image* (London: Jonathan Cape, 1947), p. 29.

[7] I. A. Richards, *The Philosophy of Rhetoric,* New York: Oxford University Press, 1936), p. 96f.

ical relationship of the two parts. Ogden and Richards further develop the idea of analogy of relationships in their *Meaning of Meaning,* stating:

> the usual metaphor is the use of reference to a group of things between which a given relation holds, for the purpose of facilitating the discrimination of an analogous relation to another group. In the understanding of metaphorical language one reference borrows part of the context of another in abstract form. [8]

Once the Doctrine of Analogy is accepted as a more complete interpretation and understanding of metaphorical expression than that offered by the Doctrine of Ornament, we are faced with the problem of how the perception of analogy which forms the metaphor is organized. We have stated that it can be a simple analogy between two concrete objects, as well as a more involved expression of analogy of relationships between the two terms. Let us illustrate more clearly the different patterns which function in a metaphor based on the perception of similarities for the purpose of exploring this type of metaphorical usage in the poetry of Carlos Pellicer.

In Pellicer's metaphors based on the Doctrine of Analogy we will examine the following types: one, an analogy between two concretes (this includes person to person, person to concrete object, object to object, etc.); two, an analogy between a concrete and an abstract (this can include a concrete object with an intangible or a concrete with a concept or an emotion); and three, an analogy between two abstracts.

The effect these types of metaphors may produce varies in terms of the relationship or relationships bared by the two figures composing the metaphor. The effectiveness of the metaphor is the standard by which we measure the genius of our poet. For the metaphor must be fresh and express something that cannot be said any other way. It may, as we will demonstrate, express a new truth because of the unique similarity uncovered by the poet. We will not cover all aspects of the effect of this metaphor for it anticipates the last type of metaphor based on a tensive relationship of its

---

[8] C. K. Ogden and I. A. Richards, *The Meaning of Meaning,* 10th ed. (London: Routledge and Kegan Paul, Ltd., 1960), p. 323.

parts. Prior to the study of Pellicer's metaphors, let us examine one more aspect of this type of metaphor.

The metaphorical imagery arising from the analogical relationship of two different figures brings forth another point of distinction between traditional poetry and modern poetry. It can be accepted that the analogy between two concretes is most easily ascertained since it is usually based on some recognizable physical characteristic or similar function. The second and third types, although admittedly more tenuous, still allow for a certain universality in interpretation. It is the area of meaning and interpretation of a given metaphor that raises a question. What are the limitations placed on the poet in selecting the figures for his analogical metaphor? Certainly newness or uniqueness of perception has been, and continues to be, a prerequisite for a good metaphor. But the quest for newness is limited by Aristotle's warning that the metaphor not be "farfetched." Therefore, we may conclude that the poet should be inventive and unique in his selection of materials for a particular image, but not so inventive that some obvious sensory quality is not present to give the image a universal meaning.

I. A. Richards responds to this problem in *Principles of Literary Criticism* when he states:

> Too much importance has always been attached to the sensory qualities of images. What gives an image efficacy is less its vividness as an image than its character as a mental event peculiarly connected with sensation.... In other words, what matters is not the sensory resemblance of an image to the sensation which is its prototype, but some other relation, at present hidden from us in the jungles of neurology. [9]

Thus for Richards the image is not only a literary device, but also a physiological phenomenon. He divides the image into two types calling one "tied" and the other "free." The first he relates to the auditory process and states that the images of this type are "among the most obvious of mental happenings. Any line of verse or prose slowly read, will, for the most people, sound mutely in the

---

[9] I. A. Richards, *Principles of Literary Criticism* (New York: A Harvest Book, 1925), pp. 119-120.

imagination somewhat as it would if read aloud." [10] Wellek and Warren support this definition of tied imagery saying that it is "auditory and muscular imagery, necessarily aroused even though one reads to oneself and approximately the same for all adequate readers." [11]

In a metaphor based on analogical comparison the "tied" image would correspond to perceiving some sensory similarities or physical likeness which would have a universal meaning to almost every reader. The perception of similarity is based on a situation which exists prior to the image, and is therefore discovered and not created by the poet. When an image transcends the sphere of perception of visual or other sensory similarities, the creative imagination of the poet and the reader are boundless. Richards calls this type of imagery "free."

In the above cited book Richards is opposed to the theory "that all attentive and sensitive readers will experience the same images...," [12] and later contends that:

> It cannot be too clearly recognized that individuals differ not only in the type of imagery which they employ, but still more in the particular images which they produce. In their whole reactions to a poem, or to a single line of it, their *free images* are the point at which two readings are most likely to differ. The fact that they differ may very well be quite immaterial. Fifty different readers will experience not one common picture but fifty different pictures. [13]

Wellek and Warren are again in accord with Richards when they say that a "free" image is "visual and else, varying much from person to person or type to type." [14]

The Spanish critic, Carlos Bousoño makes a historical distinction calling the tied image "imagen tradicional" and the free image "imagen contemporánea." In the first, says Bousoño,

> la semejanza entre sus dos planos se basa siempre en una condición objetiva (física, moral, o axiológica) que es *pre-*

---

[10] Richards, *Principles,* p. 120.
[11] Rene Wellek and Austin Warren, *Theory of Literature,* 3rd ed. (New York: Harcourt, Brace and World, 1956), p. 187.
[12] Richards, *Principles,* p. 121.
[13] Richards, *Principles,* pp. 123-124.
[14] Wellek and Warren, p. 187.

> *via* al sujeto que las contempla y de tan abultado relieve
> que en cuanto éste se pone frente a aquélla no tiene más
> remedio que aceptarla. [15]

As for the "imagen contemporánea" we perceive another phenomenon in which

> la semejanza objetiva entre los dos planos es perceptible
> tras el esfuerzo de un sutil análisis; pero —obsérvese—
> sólo es visible tras ese esfuerzo, no antes, no en la lectura
> espontánea del instante poético en cuestión.... [16]

The modern poet who makes use of the "free" or "contemporary" image is not bound by Aristotle's warning that the metaphor not be "farfetched." For what objective criteria can there
be to judge the "appropriateness" of a metaphor? The poet's task
is, according to C. Day-Lewis, to exert some form of control over
the material world. This material world in the modern era has
created a need for an ever-expanding and far-reaching metaphor.
Day-Lewis advises: "If a 20th century poet belabors us with pistons
and engines, pylons and dialectics we must bear with him; for he
is about the poet's business, perhaps ineptly, of bringing order
out of confusion." [17] Thus the analogy which forms the metaphor,
no matter how "unpoetic" or obscure it may appear, is the poet's
attempt to reconcile XXth century matter with a poetic spirit.

---

[15] Carlos Bousoño, *Teoría de la expresión poética,* 4th ed. (Madrid: Gredos, 1966), p. 108.

[16] Bousoño, pp. 110-111. He continues: "Para la sensibilidad del lector,
es, pues, como si tal semejanza no existiera, y por eso comencé por negarla.
Nuestra emoción es independiente y previa al reconocimiento intelectual del
parecido objetivo, que sólo alcanzamos a vislumbrar después, si ellos nos
complace, con la ulterior reflexión la cual se hace superflua desde el punto
de vista estrictamente estético.

En la metáfora tradicional ocurre justamente al revés: en ella el reconocimiento intelectual de la semejanza objetiva es anterior y condición ne-
cesaria de toda posible emoción poética, pues precisamente ésta depende
de aquél... en la imagen tradicional la semejanza objetiva y su conocimiento
por el lector es su *modificante extrínseco,* mientras que no lo es en la imagen
visionaria, cuyo modificante extrínseco consiste en el sentimiento (no el
conocimiento) por parte del lector del parecido *emocional,* y no del parecido
objetivo."

[17] Day-Lewis, p. 104.

Along with the aforementioned criteria for analyzing Pellicer's metaphors, our observations will include a consideration of the modernity of these metaphors, e.g. his use of the "free" or "contemporary" image.

B. Analogy Between Two Concretes

The metaphors which combine person to person or person to object are indeed rare in Pellicer's poetry. His involvement with the world around him, the world of things, virtually excluded poems about people (his later works, especially his religious poems are an exception). Metaphors of the first type, person to person are limited to a few of Bolívar, "escultor desta América" (56), and several "anti-Yanqui" barbs in which the North Americans appear as a "truculento plato de ladrones" (76) or a "líder técnico del deshonor" (84); or as "bárbaros" (90); and finally in a combination of anti-materialist and anti-Yankee sentiment as a "rey de fonógrafo." (91)

The metaphor of the second variety, analogy between a person and an object is only slightly more frequent. In the initial poem of *Piedra de Sacrificios* he refers to the heroes of Latin America as "hombres de diamante," transferring both the precious and durable connotations of a diamond to describe the characteristics of these men. A far more original and modern use of this same type of metaphor is found in the second poem of the same book:

> Uxmal,
> tú llenaste mi corazón,
> y tu raza culta es mi alegría
> y mi vaso sincero de pasión. (67)

Here a race of people is described in terms of a glass from which the poet derives joy, inspiration and spiritual nourishment. This class of metaphor runs the risk of being too obvious and at times rhetorical — "Popocatéptl, monarca de los Andes mexicanos," (91) but Pellicer utilizes it for some light and unique images of the moon:

> Frente a las vertiginosas mercaderías
> la Luna es una viuda pobre
> y la Aurora una huérfana chiquillería. (81)

¡La luna como una joven bañada
con su perfume silencioso
y su inmensa mirada!   (124)

Nombremos a la luna
alguacila de rondas de los cánticos.

El infinito astrónomo
no es más que un viejo verde
que le echa encima desbordado anteojo.   (303)

and a game of perception:

El río allá es un niño y aquí un hombre.   (303)

By far the largest number of metaphors in our first area of
classification derive from analogies between two concretes other
than persons. A metaphor of this type will have one of two possible results: one, there will be a transference of meaning from
one term to the other (which would give the traditional definition
of metaphor as "something in terms of something else"); or two,
the two terms will interact without a loss of individual characteristics to produce either a third term, or a visual, intellectual or
emotive effect. In this part of our analysis we will stress principally
the first result since the second will fall into a category of later
discussion.

Certainly the most obvious metaphors of this class, those which
lend themselves to facile interpretations are those which seek a
visible link between the two terms. Some of Pellicer's early poems
reveal these types of metaphors: "La nave/es ave rara" (24) in
which a phonic analogy, as well as the physical resemblance of
sails to wings, is exploited. The metaphor "la luna corta y cortante/
era el único fruto de una gigantesca fronda" relies on the roundness
of the two terms for its transference of meaning. A similar action
is seen in the metaphors "cuerno de la luna" (48); "los triángulos
de la cordillera" (69); "la tela del cielo" (27); "basílicas de los
cantiles vastos" (266); "Como árboles... mis brazos se levantaron"
(66); and "Tus edificios suben como los árboles del trópico" (217).
In addition to being obvious, metaphors of this type have a short
life span and quickly become museum pieces such as: "el gigantesco globo del cielo" (183); or they can degenerate to pure cliché:
"queso de la luna" (78).

The above metaphors do not rise above a descriptive function. They are in a true sense ornamentation and nothing more. We are not using the term description in an absolutely negative sense, but only if that description is puerile or stale. Pellicer demonstrates that this type of metaphor can reach truly poetic heights. In his "Aviation poems" of *Piedra...*, he offers a fresh view of reality as seen from a plane: "El Pao de Assucar era un espantapájaros/ soberbio" (77) and,

> El mar de Río de Janeiro
> es una antigua barcarola
> que está aprendiendo la ola
> leve de mi pensamiento. (78)

and finally,

> Tu mar y tu montaña
> —un puñadito de Andes y mil litros de
>   Atlántico—, (79)

From a mere transference of visible properties, he moves this metaphor to seek out similarities in actions as well:

> gruesas ruedas de olas redobladas de
>   viento (30)
> ... ...
> El huracán que rompe sus caracoles,
> detiene sus ciegas locomotoras (115)

Here the hurricane's force is described in terms of the power of a locomotive, and, in addition there is a transference of the physical properties of the locomotive to the intangible hurricane. In a reversal of this process we have:

> El motor que perfora el aire espeso
> algo tiene de bólido y de toro. (77)

in which an airplane motor is lifted to poetic heights in its combination with the shooting star (rapidity) and the bull (power).

Pellicer employs this form of metaphor to create some of his most unique and creacionist images:

El cielo de los Andes
es una agua divina que se ha echado a
    volar   (69)
... ...
tu cuerpo es de caoba   (108)
... ...
Sólo el árbol pirú, primo de sauce   (283)
... ...
El mar noche es la rana gigantesca:
croa gárgaras bruscas en las rocas.   (265)

There is a sense of daring, as well as security in his artistic ability.
He casts off the pointing "como" and allows the metaphors to reveal
themselves. "Estudio" (*Hora y 20*) which is composed exclusively
by means of metaphors of this category demonstrates the degree of
his advancement. From timid beginnings which feared to stray from
a verisimilitude of an objective reality, he strikes out in an auda-
cious and imaginative display of poetic prowess:

Esta fuente no es más que el varillaje
de la sombrilla
que hizo andrajos el viento.
Estas flores no son más que un poco de agua
llena de confeti.
Estas palomas son pedazos de papel
en el que no escribí hace poco tiempo.
Esa nube es mi camisa
que se llevó el viento.
Esa ventana es un agujero
discreto o indiscreto.
¿El viento? Acaba de pasar un tren
con demasiados pasajeros...
Este cielo ya no le importa a nadie;
esa piedra es su equipaje. Lléveselo.
Nadie sabe donde estoy
ni por qué han llegado así
las asonancias y los versos.   (186)

C. ANALOGY BETWEEN A CONCRETE ELEMENT
AND AN ABSTRACT OR INTANGIBLE

Here, as in the previous category, the metaphor will exhibit
either transference or interaction. In this part of our discussion
we will emphasize the former.

The metaphor of this type may have a purely descriptive function as seen in the following:

> [La tarde] se hila
> la red sutil de un rayo de Luna espectral   (22)
> ... ...
> Septiembre es ese hombre que está echando
>   sus redes
> melancólicamente   (27)

But instances of a purely descriptive function for this type of metaphor are rare. Pellicer is not a poet who can deal with abstracts, generalized statements or concepts. His poetic reality must be touched, felt, seen or sensed in some manner if it is to exist at all. That is why the majority of the metaphors combining an abstract or an intangible with a concrete object transfer the qualities of the latter to the former. "Esta doncella es bella como mi fe," (87) and "el mar semejante a un tranquilo secreto," (30) are infrequent exceptions which employ the converse transfer of indefinite qualities to concrete objects.

1. *Transference of Concrete Object to Emotions*

In "el diamante de amor" (9) he compares God's love to a diamond which transfers its connotations of value, brilliance and durability to the emotion love. Likewise, in "la gota perenne de una estrella/sobre la estalactita de la esperanza," (71) hope is revealed as small (gota) but constant and likened to the slow continual process of forming a stalactite. And finally he reverses the metaphor of God's love when he refers to carnal love: "Amor es barro y odio es de diamante." (132) As the reader can note, abstract concepts such as love, hope, and hate, which are meaningless due to their generality, are transformed by the metaphors so that their particular significance can be experienced by the reader. They are not explicative, but rely on their ability to arouse an intellectual or an emotional response from the reader.

2. *Transference of a Concrete Object to an Abstract Concept or
an Intangible*

Memory for Pellicer is not something relegated a place in the
past, but rather is a constant force in the present. Here he emphasizes its presence by giving it physical mass through metaphor:

> Me reclino en tu recuerdo
> como en el talle de una palmera   (104)

and again,

> Los nombres se olvidan poco a poco
> bajo la estrella reinante del
> collar de tu recuerdo   (177)

Silence is not the mere absence of sound, but a visible presence:

> tu silencio
> que era como una niebla   (108)

and

> aludido diamante fue el silencio   (91)

Absence is heightened by its analogical link with the desert, "desierto de tu ausencia" (104). Time is a container which holds the
past: "sus meditaciones proféticas/ disbordaron el vaso oscuro del
tiempo" (170-171). And a look leaves the boundaries of passive
sight to become a creative object in "vivo pincel de una mirada" (89).

Pellicer's poetry, we have stated and will repeat again, is a
highly personal and creative interpretation of a reality that because
of the weakness of words, has become static and generalized. Pellicer's metaphors recreate this reality to his personal vision and the
metaphor in this category is highly instrumental in achieving
that end.

3. *Analogy Between Two Abstracts*

From our previous comments on Pellicer's metaphorical expression the reader might deduce that this type of metaphor appears

infrequently in his work. Pellicer is uncomfortable when he cannot see or touch his poetic elements. Thus some of his early experiments with this metaphor fall into mere ornamentation, for example, "La vida era tan bella como el amanecer" (13) or "Su cortesía,/un aire de magnolias sobre el camino de la selva" (170). However his later poetry utilizes this technique to create some of his most modern metaphors in the sense of their multiple effects and tensive character. He avoids familiarity or objectifying death by saying it "Es el sagrado elemento, el fluido del tránsito,/la inmensa fe muda" (209). The feeling of solitude, an inexpressible state, is evoked from the reader in metaphors rich in their tensive interaction: "Porque la soledad es el olvido/y el recuerdo totales , ... " (258). Here are metaphors that rebuke interpretation — they must be felt if they are to exist at all.

D. The Verbal Metaphor

The metaphors discussed to this point have all been composed of two nouns joined in an analogical relationship either by aposition, the preposition "of," or some form of the verb "to be" or an equivalent. In this category we are going to deal with those metaphors in which the noun is changed metaphorically because of an expressed verbal relationship. The principal difference between the metaphor composed of two nouns and the verbal metaphor resides in the nature of the change which takes place. In the first type of metaphor such as "el cuerno de la luna" there is an immediate analogy between physical characteristics of the two terms and therefore a transference of these characteristics. On the other hand the metaphor, "la torre de Estambul cazó luceros" implies the comparison "como el hombre cazó pájaros," thus personifying the tower. Unlike the first metaphor, there is no transference indicated within the terms composing the metaphor. Thus the first type of metaphor reveals the relationship that exists between the two terms while the second, the verbal metaphor, suggests a possible analogical relationship.

The verbal metaphor appears in the earliest of Pellicer's poems. In these initial experiments with this form we note two functions: one, a descriptive function with the purpose of animating an otherwise static scene:

> Y el alba al encender
> en gran faro del día   (13)
> ... ...
> el día jugó su as de oro
> y lo perdió en tanto azul   (16)
> ... ...
> Al desplomar la sombra su silueta
> se desplumaba el cielo en nubes largas   (25)
> ... ...
> su dinamita la tempestad   (49)

the second, and more frequent function, is for personification:

> La mañana,
> afilaba vibrantes espadines
> entre los árboles de sombra aldeana.   (25)
> ... ...
> cuando la noche nos invadió   (51)
> ... ...
> Una nube peinó de sombra suave
> la bahía , . . .   (79)
> ... ...
> la luz alerta caza nubes   (187)

The verbal metaphor as personification produces some humorous images as well: "Las palmeras ... andaban de compras" (75) and "Los molinos piensan en la aviación académicamente" (179).

As Pellicer's poetry develops, the verbal metaphor becomes a sophisticated tool which shapes a number of challenging images such as:

> Baila el silencio en la onda movida,
> buen bailarín
> en tonos libres y actitud oída.   (227)

in which the synesthetic element coupled with the implied verbal analogy extends the effect into various sensual levels. The later experiments with verbal metaphors reveal a search for precision in expression not characteristic of earlier works. In the metaphor:

> Y la divina poesía,
> como en las bodas de Canaan,
> hechiza el agua . . . .   (182)

poetry is not only personified by the verb "hechiza" but is endowed with a magical and spiritual quality which can convert reality. The verb "desnuda" in "el sol desnuda el cielo" (283), personifies and animates the scene, and lends connotations of purity and solitude as well. At times Pellicer creates a verb to create an image which alone can evoke the mood he wants to communicate: "En palabras de amor paloma el día" (288).

Thus his verbal metaphors, as those discussed earlier, show an evolution from fairly traditional functions of description, animation, and expression of relationships, to a more complicated and precise desire to communicate personal feelings, capture a sensation or evoke a particular mood. Although many of the different types of metaphors discussed above possess characteristics which we termed modern, it is the tensive metaphor that most accurately represents the modern's achievement in metaphorical expression. Prior to examination of the tensive metaphor in Pellicer's poetry, let us examine several theories on the subject.

F.   The Tensive Metaphor

As witnessed by the varied attempts to define the metaphor in modern poetry, general disapproval with Aristotelian concepts is characteristic of XXth century criticism. There is a definite movement away from treating metaphor as a literary device for ornamentation or ennobling the poetic object; likewise the poet is not content to merely seek similarities between the two elements of his metaphor. Richards, in explaining his tenor-vehicle concept, stresses that the interaction of the two may consist of "disparates" as well as "resemblances." [18] Later he adds: "As the two things put together are *more remote*, the tension created is, of course, greater." [19] It is the tensive character of the metaphor, a note struck in our earlier discussion of metaphor in symbolism, that has received much critical attention in the XXth century. Likewise it is the tensive relationship of the tenor and vehicle that best aids in understanding metaphorical usage in Pellicer's poetry.

---

[18] Richards, *Philosophy of Rhetoric*, p. 108.
[19] Richards, *Philosophy of Rhetoric*, p. 125.

1. *Critical Explanations of Tension*

Allen Tate considers the element of tension not only essential to the function of metaphor, but to all of poetry. "The meaning of poetry," says Tate, "is its 'tension,' the full organized body of all the extension and intension we can find in it." [20]

Ruth Herschberger narrows the effect of tension to metaphor, but treats it as if it were some magical, undecipherable element:

> Now, in a metaphor it is true that some aspects of objects alluded to are ignored; the aim is to include only as many attributes as can contribute to the sense of congruence, and plausibility. On the other hand, mere "easy" abstraction of likeness does not produce a metaphor. This is where the anomalous factor of "tension" comes in . . . [21]

We could cite numerous examples of the word "tension" as it appears in discussions of metaphor, but let us study two critics for whom the element of tension is the core of metaphorical expression: Phillip Wheelwright and Octavio Paz.

Wheelwright first proposed his theories in *The Burning Fountain* in which the opening paragraph of the chapter "Metaphoric Tension" makes this assertion:

> It should be clear by now that metaphor in its radical, which is to say its semantic sense, is much more than a grammatical maneuver or rhetorical stratagem. The essence of metaphor consists in the nature of the tension which is maintained among the heterogeneous elements brought together in one commanding image or expression. [22]

Wheelwright discusses various applications of the term "tension" with particular emphasis on Martin Foss's theory of "energy-tension" which calls for the "mutual destruction" of the individual terms of the metaphor by which "new and strange insight arises." [23]

---

[20] Allen Tate, *On the Limits of Poetry* (New York: The Swallow Press and William Morrow and Company, 1948), p. 83.

[21] Ruth Herschberger, "Structure of Metaphor," *The Kenyon Review* 5, No. 3 (Summer, 1943), p. 434.

[22] Phillip Wheelwright, *The Burning Fountain* (Bloomington, Indiana: Indiana University Press, 1959), p. 101.

[23] Wheelwright, p. 104.

Wheelwright objects to the idea of "mutual destruction" in Foss's definition. He asks: "If the conventional meanings of the terms drawn into the energy-tension were really destroyed, would not the tension cease to exist?" [24] He proposes instead Vasconcelos's concept of tensive metaphor as "vital synthesis" which consists of "a unification of heterogeneous elements in which the heterogeneity is yet paradoxically preserved." [25]

He then offers his hypothesis that "metaphor at its best tends to achieve fullness of semantic energy-tension by a merging of two complementary elements — *simile* and *plurisignation*." [26] In the first, he contends, "two verbal expressions each conveying an individual image or idea, are joined; in plurisignation, a single verbal expression carries two or more meanings simultaneously." [27] These two elements are not independent of each other, but "blend into a metaphoric unity-in-diversity." [28] A complementary exposition of this idea is found in Octavio Paz's *El arco y la lira.*

The poem, says Octavio Paz quite succinctly, is language in tension. [29] A poetic image which according to Paz goes through a dialectical process can have one of three ends: the first term may replace the second; the first term may lose its significance due to the strength of the second; or "los dos elementos aparecen frente a frente irreductibles hostiles." [30] It is this third possibility that best describes, in Paz's terms, the tensive metaphor. Each of the elements of this type of metaphor bring with it a unique and heterogeneous reality. Take for example the metaphor "the shriek of yellow": shriek belongs to the realm of sound and yellow to a visible reality, but the result of the tension between the two creates the third and most important reality — that of the poem. This is the essence of poetry for Octavio Paz, presentation of reality and not representation. Meaning is not found outside of the poem, but is the poem itself. "El poeta no quiere decir: *dice.*" [31] He makes a distinction

---

[24] Wheelwright, p. 105.
[25] Wheelwright, p. 105.
[26] Wheelwright, p. 106.
[27] Wheelwright, p. 106.
[28] Wheelwright, p. 106.
[29] Octavio Paz, *El arco y la lira* (Mexico: Fondo de Cultura Económica, 1956), p. 106.
[30] Paz, *El arco y la lira,* p. 91.
[31] Paz, *El arco y la lira,* p. 105.

between meaning to say something (representation) and saying it (presentation):

> Cuando tropezamos con una sentencia oscura decimos: "Lo que quieren decir estas palabras es esto o aquello". Y para decir "esto o aquello" recurrimos a otras palabras. Toda frase quiere decir algo que puede ser dicho o explicado por otra frase. En consecuencia, el sentido o significado es un *querer decir*. O sea: un decir que puede decirse de otra manera. El sentido de la imagen, por el contrario, es la imagen misma: no se puede decir con otras palabras. *La imagen se explica a sí misma*. Nada, excepto ella, puede decir lo que quiere decir. Sentido e imagen son la misma cosa. Un poema no tiene más sentido que sus imágenes. [32]

This statement by Paz captures the spirit and essence of the battle of modern art: the freeing of the metaphor and poetry from the limitations of some exterior reality. The metaphor no longer has to strive for verisimilitude nor measure up to something outside of itself. The only criteria one can use to judge it is its effectiveness within the poem. By recognizing the power of the metaphor in which the two parts are in a tensive relationship, we no longer demand that it explain something. For as Paz states: "La imagen no explica: invita a recrearla y, literalmente, a revivirla." [33] Where the neoclassic and romantic metaphor were limited by their need to say something in terms of an existing reality, thereby abstracting their idea or emotion, the modern uses the metaphor to recreate the particular experience and invite the reader to participate in the act. This type of metaphor is certainly more difficult for as Brooks points out, the modern poet demands that the "reader use his imagination to fill in the apparent blanks in logic." [34] Difficulty not withstanding, a patient and dedicated reader will benefit the reward of his endeavors.

We have avoided drawing attention to the obvious similarities that exist between the ideas of the proponents of the theory of tensive metaphor and those of Bergson, Vasconcelos and the symbolist poets. Such comments would not only be superfluous but

---

[32] Paz, *El arco y la lira,* p. 104.
[33] Paz, *El arco y la lira,* p. 107.
[34] Brooks, p. xxiv.

would run the risk of being misleading. But although direct influence may be difficult to pinpoint, we can be assured that neither Wheelwright nor Paz developed in a cultural vacuum. They were certainly aware of the theories and experimentations of the symbolists, as well as the debt modern poetry owes to the baroque era. Their ideas represent an extension and development of those ideas as they seem appropriate and relevant to a modern poetic.

Let us now return to Pellicer and examine how the theory of the tensive metaphor functions in his poetry.

2. *The Tensive Metaphor in Pellicer*

An analysis of this type of metaphor seems contradictory to all we have been saying of the modern metaphor — that it defies literal interpretation, that it states something that can't be said in any other way, that it doesn't mean, it exists. While we admit these statements to be true, we feel obligated to do more than list a series of tensive metaphors and allow them to speak for themselves. For this also would be an injustice. The metaphors should be studied not as separate entities but in the total context of the poem. Indeed the reader, to appreciate their effectiveness, their emotive charge, should have at his disposal the entire work in which they exist. Our method we hope will serve as a compromise to a mere catalogue of isolated metaphors and the unworkable (at least within the scope of the present study) format of an annoted anthology. Our purpose, in this analysis, is two-fold: one, to demonstrate the various ways by which tension is created and the end that it serves; and second, to contend that this type of metaphor most clearly illustrates the modern achievement of poetry.

One of modern poetry's most valuable contributions to metaphorical expression was to restore and bring to prominence the notion that successful metaphors need not rely on an association of similarities, but, quite the contrary, are often times most expressive when they link contrary, and apparently contradictory terms.

We find that Pellicer employs this technique to express emotions that are inexpressible in words. Thus he joins a word with its opposite in order that their individual meanings are lost and what emerges is the vehicle to experience the particular emotion. The feeling of solitude is expressed as: "Tu soledad gigantesca/como la plentitud de tus campos" (157). Here the feeling of solitude or absence is heightened by its tensive relationship to plenitude. What comes forth is not a description of solitude, or a statement on solitude, but the feeling of solitude. In "soledad, cárcel abierta" (212) solitude as a jail is intensified since it is confinement without physical restraints. In like manner he expresses anguish as "el brillo de la angustia" (196), a feeling so terrible, so ever present, so powerful, that it shines. He destroys any preconceived idea we may have about the feeling of anguish by forcing us to experience it as he feels it. Again in "un día sinfónicamente mudo" (136) he avoids statement in favor of experience. Here is, as Bergson stated, intuition of reality that cannot be expressed, only evoked by a combination of contraries. Poetry which we logically assume is verbal expression, in Pellicer becomes "la silenciosa/música de callar un sentimiento" (268). In a poem from *Piedra* . . . dedicated to Uxmal, an ancient Mayan city, he writes:

> Uxmal,
> llena de ingenieros poéticos,
> opulenta y sepulcral. (66)

He expresses the emotive force that Uxmal generates: a city made of rock which has not seen life for centuries is at the same time opulent for glorious achievements that are contained in its history vibrating in the rocks. Opulent as well for the wealth of inspiration and pride it contains for the modern dwellers of the land of the Mayas who rediscover its treasures.

A similar method for creating a tensive metaphor discussed briefly in an earlier chapter is the union of two unlike or disparate elements in one image. At times the relationship is easily ascertained as in:

> Elemental, la mano enriquecida
> rayó el agua al diamante y echó *al fuego*
> *del poema,* las fuerzas de la vida. (210, underlining
> mine)

where the archetypal image of fire as a purifying element is transferred to the poem which strives for the same cleansing effect. He employs the same idea in a later poem when he writes:

> Yo quiero arder mis pies en los braseros
> de la angustia más sola,
> para salir desnudo hacia el poema   (256)

Here again it is purification by fire ("braseros"), but only this time it is linked to an emotion "angustia." These are not the best examples of a method of tensive metaphor for the meaning is derived not from the context of the poem, but in previous symbolic meaning for the term "fuego."

A better example is found in the aforementioned poem "Uxmal" where he says:

> Por tu divina sensación
> se alza una voz,
> se alza otra voz:
> Uxmal,
> desde *las rocas de mi corazón.*   (65, emphasis
>   mine)

If one were to interpret this metaphor by referring to the physical characteristic of a stone, its hardness, or even interpret it as referring to depth, he would miss the point. "Rocas" here refer to the stone temples and pyramids and make no statement, but rather reveal the relationship, or more accurately, the interpenetration that exists between the poet and his subject, Uxmal.

The danger of approaching these metaphors with preconceived ideas is evident in:

> Vuelvo a encender la *luna de tu amor*
> sobre mis labios trágicos   (157, emphasis
>   mine)

where "luna de tu amor" seems to be a fairly traditional, romantic metaphor. But the context of the poem and its relationship to the verb "encender" reveal otherwise. When he speaks of "lighting the moon," the light of the moon is not direct light, but rather a reflective one, the presence of love is not a direct one, but a reflective, remembered one, made real only by the "labios trágicos."

Similarly a metaphor such as "flor de viaje" (174) does not reach its full tensive potential unless taken in context with the poem in which it appears and other poems where Pellicer speaks of the futility of travel as a means of escaping or forgetting. The idea of travel for that purpose has, like the flower, promise of beauty, of fruit, of some lasting quality, but it, as does the flower, soon withers and fades under the persistent presence of memory.

At times an image such as "trescientas olas automóviles" (262) seems absurd in its illogical joining of waves and automobiles in which one noun is apparently modifying another. But the appropriateness and lucidity of the image becomes apparent when we realize that the author is writing his poem of the sea in the midst of an urban center. Thus "olas automóviles" is the simultaneous presence of memory and matter, past and present. He purposely avoids making one of the terms an adjectival form for that would presume a blending which is contrary to the desired effect of the simultaneity of two distinct impressions.

A tensive metaphor, in Wheelwright's idea of plurisignation, can be found in what is seemingly an obvious metaphor based on an analogy of physical similarities such as in: "tambor pulido/desta columna rota" (173). Is the poet simply describing a broken column of Greek ruins in terms of the roundness of a drum? That is one level of interpretation certainly. But if he reads it in context the plurisignation of the metaphor emerges:

> ¿Por qué la mano lenta sobre el tambor
> pulido
> desta columna rota, tórridamente va?

The apparent contradiction of "mano lenta" and "tórridamente va" reveals why the poet chose "tambor" as a comparison to "columna." The column, as does the drum, reverberates with rhythms; rhythms which reveal to the poet the treasures of the Classical past. And the hand passes over the column slowly, yet torridly, because it is the immediate receiver of the vibrant messages.

These metaphors are not facile creations. They demand the reader's attention, participation, and at times his recreation. Metaphors whose logical links are conspicuously absent, such as "Aguas verticales, horizontal, cerámica y primera" (208), and "Nuestras palabras, como plantas/atlánticas que el pañuelo del aire/abandonó en todas las playas" (157) can be summarily dismissed as unintelligible, private and obscure. But the persistent and resourceful reader will experience the pleasure of participating in the writer's creative act. He will not be a passive receptacle who is told what to see and what to feel, but an active participant who will see and feel for himself.

The tensive metaphor illustrates clearly the modern advances of metaphorical expression. Let us summarize some of the achievements. The metaphor in modern poetry is liberated from an objective, exterior reality. The only reality of real import is the poetic reality of the poem. The world of the poem is unique and autonomous.

The modern metaphor is free of *a priori* limitations such as verisimilitude, truth, decorum, appropriateness, etc. It is judged solely on its effectiveness within the reality of the poem.

Finally it solidifies and advances the struggle against language. It is a criticism of its own means of expression. It rebels against abstract expression, general statements, useless rhetoric, loose sentimentality. In short, it attempts to liberate poetry from the word, and make language once again serve poetry.

BIBLIOGRAPHY

A. General

Abrams, M. H. *The Mirror and the Lamp.* New York: Oxford University Press, 1953.

Alazraki, Jaime. *Poética y poesía de Pablo Neruda.* New York: Las Americas, 1965.

Alonso, Amado. *Materia y forma en poesía.* Madrid: Gredos, 1965.

————. *Poesía y estilo de Pablo Neruda.* Buenos Aires: Sudamericana, 1966.

Alonso, Dámaso. *Poesía española.* 3rd ed. Madrid: Gredos, 1957.

Asunción Silva, José. *Prosas y versos.* Mexico: Editorial Cultura, 1942.

Babbitt, Irving. *Rousseau and Romanticism.* 6th ed. Cambridge, Massachusetts: Houghton-Mifflin, 1930.

Balakian, Anna. *Literary Origins of Surrealism: A New Mysticism in French Poetry.* New York: King's Crown Press, 1947.

Barrett, William. *Irrational Man: A Study in Existential Philosophy.* Garden City, New York: Doubleday and Company, Inc., 1962.

Bate, Walter Jackson. *From Classic to Romantic.* New York: Harper and Row, 1961.

Baudelaire, Charles Pierre. *Intimate Journals.* Introduction by T. S. Eliot. London: Blackamore Press, 1930.

————. *Oeuvres Completes de Baudelaire.* Belgium: Bibliotheque de la Pleiade, 1951.

————. *Baudelaire as a Literary Critic.* Edited by Lois Boe Hyslop and Francis E. Hyslop Hr. University Park, Pennsylvania: Pennsylvania State University Press, 1963.

Bayn, Max I. "The Present State of the Study of Metaphor." *Books Abroad.* Vol. 35, No. 3. (Summer 1961), pp. 215-219.

Beal, George Denton. *Modern Theories of the Metaphorical Mode of Expression.* Ph. D. Dissertation. Pittsburgh: University of Pittsburgh, 1949.

Beguin, Albert. *El alma romántica y el sueño.* Mexico: Fondo de Cultura Económica, 1954.

Bergson, Henri. *Laughter.* Translated by Cloudesley Brereton and Fred Rothwell. New York: The Macmillan Company, 1928.

————. *Selections from Bergson.* Ed. Harold A. Larrabee. New York: Appleton-Century-Crofts, 1949.

Bertocci, Angelo Phillip. *From Symbolism to Baudelaire.* Carbondale: Southern Illinois University Press, 1964.

Blackmur, R. P. *Form and Value in Modern Poetry.* Garden City, New York: Doubleday and Co., Inc., 1957.

Borges, Jorge Luis, *Leopoldo Lugones.* Buenos Aires: Editorial Troquel, 1955.

Bousoño, Carlos. *Teoría de la expresión poética.* 4th ed. Madrid: Biblioteca Romántica Hispánica, 1966.

Bowra, C. M. *The Heritage of Symbolism*. London: Macmillan and Company, Ltd., 1947.

————. *The Romantic Imagination*. Cambridge, Massachusetts: Harvard University Press, 1949.

Brooks, Cleanth. *Modern Poetry and the Tradition*. Chapel Hill, North Carolina: University of North Carolina Press, 1967.

————, and Warren, Robert Penn. *Understanding Poetry*. 3rd ed. New York: Holt, Rinehart and Winston, Inc., 1961.

Capsas, Cleon Wade. *The Poetry of Jorge Luis Borges, 1923-1963*. Ph.D. Dissertation. The University of New Mexico, 1964.

Carter, Boyd G. *Las revistas literarias de Hispanoamérica*. Mexico: Ediciones de Andrea, 1959.

Ceide-Echevarría, Gloria. *El haiku en la lírica mexicana*. Mexico: Ediciones de Andrea, 1967.

Cirlot, Juan Eduardo. *Diccionario de los ismos*. Barcelona: Editorial Argos, S. A., 1966.

Cook, Albert. *Prisms: Studies in Modern Literature*. Bloomington, Indiana: Indiana University Press, 1967.

Crane, R. S. *The Language of Criticism and the Structure of Poetry*. Toronto: University of Toronto Press, 1953.

————, ed. *Critics and Criticism*. Chicago: The University of Chicago Press, 1957.

Croce, Benedetto. *Aesthetic as Science of Expression and General Linguistic*. Translated by Douglas Ainslie; New York: Noonday Press, 1962.

Darío, Rubén. *Poesías completas*. 10th ed. Madrid: Aguilar, 1967.

de Ullman, Stephen. "Romanticism and Synesthesia." *PMLA*, LX, 3, Sept. 1945, pp. 811-827.

Deutsch, Babette. *Poetry in Our Time*. New York: Henry Holt and Company, 1952.

Eliot, T. S. ed. *Literary Essays of Ezra Pound*. Norfolk, Connecticut: New Directions, 1954.

Embler, Weller. *Metaphor and Meaning*. Deland, Florida: Everett Edwards, Inc., 1966.

Empson, William. *Seven Types of Ambiguity*. London: Chatto and Windus, 1956.

Engelberg, Edward, ed. *The Symbolist Poem*. New York: E. P. Dutton and Co., Inc., 1967.

Feder, Lillian. *Ancient Myth in Modern Poetry*. Princeton: Princeton University Press, 1971.

Foss, Martin. *Symbol and Metaphor in Human Experience*. Princeton: Princeton University Press, 1949.

Franco, Jean. *An Introduction to Spanish-American Literature*. Cambridge: Cambridge University Press, 1969.

Friedrich, Hugo. *Estructura de la lírica moderna*. Barcelona: Ed. Seix-Barral, 1959.

Frye, Northrop. *Anatomy of Criticism: Four Essays*. Princeton: Princeton University Press, 1957.

Gilson, Etienne and Thomas Langan. *A History of Philosophy: Modern Philosophy*. New York: Random House, 1964.

González Martínez, Enrique. *Antología de su obra poética*. Ed. Jaime Torres Bodet. Mexico: Fondo de Cultura Económica, 1971.

Hamburger, Michael. *The Truth of Poetry: Tensions in Modern Poetry from Baudelaire to the Nineteen-sixties.* New York: Harcourt, Brace Jovanovich, Inc., 1969.

Hanna, Thomas, ed. *The Bergsonian Heritage.* New York: Columbia University Press, 1962.

Henríquez Ureña, Max. *Breve historia del modernismo.* 2nd ed., Mexico: Fondo de Cultura Económica, 1962.

Henríquez Ureña, Pedro. *Plenitud de América.* Buenos Aires: Peña, del Guidice-Editores, 1952.

————. *Literary Currents in Hispanic America.* New York: Russell and Russell, 1963.

Hernández Luna, Juan, ed. *Conferencias del Ateneo.* Mexico: Universidad Nacional Autónoma de México, 1962.

Hershberger, Ruth. "Structure of Metaphor." *The Kenyon Review,* V, 3, Summer, 1943.

Howe, Irving. *Literary Modernism.* Greenwich, Connecticut: Fawcett Publications, Inc., 1967.

Hughes, Glenn. *Imagism and the Imagists.* New York: The Humanities Press, 1960.

Huidobro, Vicente. *Antología.* Ed. Eduardo Anguita. Santiago de Chile: Zig-Zag Editores, 1945.

————. *Obras completas de Vicente Huidobro.* Two volumes. Ed. Braulio Arenas. Santiago de Chile: Zig-Zag Editores, 1964.

————. *Poesía y Prosa: Antología.* 2nd ed. Madrid: Aguilar, S. A. de Ediciones, 1967.

Hulme, T. E. *Speculations: Essays on Humanism and the Philosophy of Art.* Ed. Herbert Read. London: Routledge and Kegan Paul Ltd., 1949.

————. *Further Speculations.* Ed. Sam Hynes. Minneapolis: University of Minnesota Press, 1955.

Isaacs, J. *The Background of Modern Poetry.* New York: E. P. Dutton and Co., Inc., 1952.

————. *An Assessment of Twentieth-Century Literature.* 2nd ed. Port Washington, New York: Kennikat Press, 1968.

Kermode, Frank. *Romantic Image.* New York: The Macmillan Co., 1957.

————, ed. *The Metaphysical Poets.* Greenwich, Connecticut: Fawcett Publications, Inc., 1969.

Krieger, Murray. *The New Apologists for Poetry.* Bloomington, Indiana: Indiana University Press, 1956.

Kumar, Shiv K. *Bergson and the Stream of Consciousness Novel.* New York: New York University Press, 1963.

Leal, Luis. "El movimiento estridentista." *Movimientos literarios de vanguardia.* Mexico: Instituto Internacional de Literatura Iberoamericana, 1965.

Lefebvre, Henri. *Introduction à la Modernité.* Paris: Les Editions de Minuit, 1962.

Lewis, C. Day. *The Poetic Image.* London: Jonathan Cape, 1947.

List Arzubide, German. *El movimiento estridentista.* Jalapa, Veracruz: Horizonte, 1929.

López Velarde, Ramón. *Obras.* Ed. José Luis Martínez. Mexico: Fondo de Cultura Económica, 1971.

Lugones, Leopoldo. *Lunario sentimental.* 3rd ed. Buenos Aires: Ediciones Centurión, 1961.

MacLeish, Archibald. *Poetry and Experience.* Baltimore: Penguin Books, 1964.

Marasso, Arturo. *Rubén Darío y su creación poética.* Buenos Aires: Biblioteca Nueva, 1946.

Micheli, Mario de. *Las vanguardias del siglo XX.* La Habana: Ediciones Unión, 1957.

Murray, J. Middleton. *The Problem of Style.* London-New York: Oxford University Press, 1922.

———. "Metaphor" in *Shakespeare Criticism 1919-35.* Ed. Bradby. New York: Oxford University Press, 1936.

Novo, Salvador. "Veinte años de literatura mexicana." *El libro y el pueblo,* IX, 4, June 1931.

Ogden, C. K., and Richards, I. A. *The Meaning of Meaning.* 10th ed. London: Routledge and Kegan Paul Ltd., 1960.

Paz, Octavio. *El arco y la lira.* Mexico: Fondo de Cultura Económica, 1956.

———. *The Labyrinth of Solitude.* New York: Grove Press, 1961.

———. *Corriente alterna.* Mexico: Siglo XXI Editores, 1967.

———. *Cuadrivio.* 2nd ed. Mexico: Joaquín Mortiz, 1969.

———. "¿Es moderna la literatura latinoamericana?" *Plural,* 1, October 1971.

Peyre, Henri, ed. *Baudelaire.* Englewood Cliffs, New Jersey: Prentice-Hall, 1962.

Poe, Edgar Allen. *Selected Writings.* Ed. E. H. Davidson. Boston: Houghton Mifflin Co., 1956.

Poggioli, Renato. *The Theory of the Avant-Garde.* Translated by Gerald Fitzgerald. Cambridge, Massachusetts: Harvard University Press, 1968.

Ponce de Hurtado, María Teresa. *El ruiseñor lleno de muerte: Aproximación a Carlos Pellicer.* Mexico: Editorial Meridiano, 1970.

Pound, Ezra. *Literary Essays.* Ed. T. S. Eliot. Norfolk, Connecticut: New Directions, 1954.

Powell, A. E. *The Romantic Theory of Poetry.* 2nd ed. New York: Russell and Russell, Inc., 1962.

Prescott, Frederick Clarke. *The Poetic Mind.* Ithaca, New York: Cornell University Press, 1959.

Raymond, Marcel. *From Baudelaire to Surrealism.* London: Methuen and Co., Ltd., 1970.

Reyes, Alfonso. *Pasado inmediato y otros ensayos.* Mexico: Colegio de México, 1941.

Richards, I. A. *Principles of Literary Criticism.* New York: A Harvest Book, 1925.

———. *The Philosophy of Rhetoric.* New York: Oxford University Press, 1936.

Rodríguez Monegal, Emir. "El retorno de las carabelas." *Revista de la Universidad de México,* XXV, 6, 1971.

Roggiano, Alfredo A. "El origen francés y la valoración hispánica del modernismo." *Influencias extranjeras en la literatura iberoamericana.* Mexico: Instituto Internacional de Literatura Iberoamericana, 1962.

———. "Luz y sombra de Leopoldo Lugones." Literary supplement of *Ovaciones* 32. Mexico: Aug. 5, 1962, p. 4.

Rosenberg, Harold. *The Tradition of the New.* New York: Grove Press, 1961.

Sainz de Robles, Federico Carlos. *Los movimientos literarios.* Madrid: Aguilar, 1957.

Schneider, Luis Mario. *El estridentismo.* Mexico: Ediciones de Bellas Artes, 1970.

Silz, Walter. *Early German Romanticism.* Cambridge, Massachusetts: Harvard University Press, 1929.

Spender, Stephen. *The Struggle of the Modern.* Berkeley and Los Angeles: University of California Press, 1963.

Spitzer, Leo. *La enumeración caótica en la poesía moderna.* Buenos Aires: Universidad de Buenos Aires, 1945.

Stead, C. K. *The New Poetic: Yeats to Eliot.* New York: Harper and Row, 1966.

Straub, William. "Conversación con Jorge Carrera Andrade," *Revista Iberoamericana,* XXXVIII, 79, April-June 1972.

Sucre, Guillermo. "Vicente Huidobro: poesía del espacio." *Imagen* 43, Feb. 15-28, 1969, pp. 6-7.

Tate, Allen. *On the Limits of Poetry.* New York: The Swallow Press and William Morrow and Co., 1948.

————. *Essays of Four Decades.* Chicago: The Swallow Press, Inc., 1959.

Thomas, Owen. *Metaphor and Related Subjects.* New York: Random House, 1969.

Torre, Guillermo de. *Historia de las literaturas de vanguardia.* Madrid: Ediciones Guadarrama, 1965.

Tuve, Rosemond. *Elizabethan and Metaphysical Imagery.* Chicago: University of Chicago Press, 1961.

Valery, Paul. *The Art of Poetry.* Translated by Denise Folliot. New York: Vintage Books, 1961.

Vasconcelos, José. *Estética.* 3rd ed. Mexico: Editorial Botas, 1945.

Videla, Gloria. *El ultraísmo: estudios sobre movimientos poéticos de vanguardia en España.* Madrid: Editorial Gredos, 1963.

Villaurrutia, Xavier. *Obras.* 2nd ed. Mexico: Fondo de Cultura Económica, 1966.

Wellek, Rene. *Concepts of Criticism.* New Haven: Yale University Press, 1965.

———— and Warren, Austin. *Theory of Literature.* New York: Harcourt, Brace and Co., 1949.

Whalley, George. *Poetic Process: An Essay in Poetics.* Cleveland: World Publishing Company, 1967.

Wheelwright, Philip. *The Burning Fountain: A Study in the Language of Symbolism.* Bloomington, Indiana: Indiana University Press, 1959.

————. *Metaphor and Reality.* Bloomington, Indiana: Indiana University Press, 1962.

Whitehead, Alfred North. *Science and the Modern World.* New York: Pelican Mentor Books, 1948.

Wilson, Edmund. *Axel's Castle.* New York: Charles Scribner's Sons, 1943.

Wimsatt, W. K., Jr. "Poetic Tension: A Summary," *The New Scholasticism,* XXXII, January 1959, pp. 132-144.

Winters, Yvon. *The Function of Criticism: Problems and Exercises.* Denver: Alan Swallow, 1957.

Wolff, Robert Paul, ed. Kant: *A Collection of Critical Essays.* Garden City, New York: Doubleday and Company, 1967.

Yurkievich, Saúl. *Modernidad de Apollinaire*. Buenos Aires: Editorial Losada, 1968.
————. *Fundadores de la nueva poesía latinoamericana*. Barcelona: Barral Editores, 1970.

B. WORKS BY CARLOS PELLICER

"Sonetos romanos," *Gladios*, I, 1 (Mexico, Jan. 1916).
"Grecia," *Gladios*, I, 2 (Mexico, Feb. 1916), p. 130.
"Prólogo a *Poemas de Antonio y Manuel Machado*." Cultura, V, 3 (Mexico, Sept. 15, 1917), pp. III-VII.
"Angel Corao; *Romanzas interiores*, Caracas," *México Moderno*, I, 8 (Mexico, Mar. 1, 1921), p. 125.
"Elim; Poemas, Santiago de Chile, 1920," *México Moderno*, I, 8 (Mexico, Mar. 1, 1921), p. 125.
"A los estudiantes mexicanos," *El Maestro*, I, 1 (Mexico, April 1, 1921), p. 37.
"Poesía," *El Maestro*, I, 2 (Mexico, May 21, 1921), pp. 201-204).
Colores en el mar y otros poemas. Mexico: Librería Cultura, 1921.
Piedra de sacrificios: Poema Iberoamericano. Mexico: Editorial Nayarit, 1924.
Seis, siete poemas. Mexico: Aztlán-Editores, 1924.
Oda de junio. Mexico: La Pajarita de Papel, 1924.
Bolívar. Mexico: Secretaría de Educación Pública, 1925.
Hora y 20. Paris: Editorial Paris-América, 1927.
Camino. Paris: Talleres de Tipografia Solsona, 1929.
5 (cinco) poemas. Supl. of Barandal. Mexico, 1931.
Esquemas para una oda tropical. Mexico: Secretaría de Relaciones.
Estrofas del mar marino. Mexico: Imprenta Mundial, 1934.
Hora de junio. Mexico: Ediciones Hipocampo, 1937.
"Ara virginum," *Revista de Literatura Mexicana*, I, 2 (Mexico, Oct.-Dec. 1940), pp. 214-225.
Recinto y otros imagenes. Mexico: Edicion Tezontle, 1941.
Exágonos. Mexico: Nueva Voz, 1941.
"Sueño dominical en la Alameda Central de la ciudad de México," *México en el arte*, 1 (Mexico, July 1948), p. 10.
Subordinaciones. Mexico: Editorial Jus, 1948.
Sonetos. Mexico: Editorial Cultura, 1950.
Práctica de vuelo. Mexico: Fondo de Cultura Económica, 1956.
Museo de Tabasco, Guía Oficial. Mexico: Instituto Nacional de Antropología e Historia, 1959.
"Introducción y antecedentes," *La pintura mural de la Revolución Mexicana*, 1921-1960. Mexico: Fondo Editorial de la Plástica Mexicana, 1960.
"Salvador Ferrando; dos rayos sobre el pintor," *Cuadernos de Bellas Artes*, II, 8 (Mexico, August 1961), p. 3.
"He olvidado mi nombre," *Sur*, 272 (Buenos Aires, Sept.-Oct. 1961), pp. 38-40.
Es un país lejano. Mexico: Foto-Ilustradores, 1961.
Material poético: 1918-1961. 2nd ed. Mexico; Universidad Nacional Autónoma de México, 1962.
Con palabras y fuego. Mexico: Fondo de Cultura Económica, 1962.

"Fuego nuevo en honor a José Clemente Orozco," *Los Sesenta* 1 (Mexico, 1964), pp. 33-38.

Teotihuacán y 13 de agosto: ruina de Tenochtitlán. Mexico: Ediciones Ecuador, 1964.

Simón Bolívar. Mexico: Secretaría de Educación Pública, 1965.

"Discurso de bienvenida," *El Despertador Americano* (Bulletin of the 2nd Congress of Latin American Writers), I, 2 (Mexico, May 1967), p. 1.

"En el centenario de Rubén Darío," *Casa de las Américas,* 42 (Havanna, May-June 1967), pp. 15-16.

"Líneas por el Che Guevara," *Cuadernos Americanos,* XXII (Mexico, Mar.-Apr. 1968), p. 105.

"Introduccion" to *Mexico,* ed. Roiter Fulvio. Zurich: Ediciones Atlantis, 1968.

"Cosilla para el nacimiento de 1967-68," *Universidad de México,* XXII, 6 (Mexico, Feb. 1968).

"Prologue" to *Muros de Luz.* Marco Antonio Flores. Mexico: Siglo XXI, 1968.

Primera antología poética. Ed. Guillermo Fernández. Mexico: Fondo de Cultura Económica, 1969.

C. STUDIES ON PELLICER

Abreu Gómez, Ermilo. *Sala de retratos.* Mexico: Editorial Leyenda, 1946.

Aguayo Spencer, Rafael. *Flor de moderna poesía mexicana.* Mexico: Libro-Mex Editores, 1955.

Aguilera-Malta, Demetrio. "Carlos Pellicer; mexicano de América," "El Gallo Ilustrado," Supl. of *El Día,* 333 (Mexico, Nov. 10, 1968), p. 4.

Aguilera, Francisco. "Pellicer, Carlos; *Exágonos," Handbook of Latin American Studies:* 1941 (Cambridge, Massachusetts, 1942), p. 456.

Ahumada, Herminio. "Homenaje a Carlos Pellicer en su cincuentenario poético," "México en la Cultura," Supl. of *Novedades,* 1037 (Mexico, Feb. 2, 1969), p. 3.

Alvarado, José. "La obra de Carlos Pellicer," *Excelsior* (Mexico, Nov. 13, 1968), p. 7-A.

Alvarez, Alfredo Juan. "La óptica del joven Pellicer, la acústica del aventurero lector," "El Gallo Ilustrado," Supl. of *El Día,* 333 (Mexico, Nov. 10, 1968), p. 2.

Anon. *"Con palabras y fuego," Tiempo,* 1129 (Mexico, 1963), p. 60.

Anon. "Escaparate de libros," "México en la Cultura," Supl. of *Novedades,* 829 (Mexico, Feb. 7, 1965), p. 8.

Anon. "Letras mexicanas; Carlos Pellicer," *Letras de Ayer y Hoy,* 1:4 (Mexico, Dec. 1965), p. 13.

Arellano, Jesús. "Las Ventas de Don Quijote," *Nivel,* 44 (Aug. 25, 1962), p. 5.

Arreola, Juan José. "Carlos Pellicer," "México en la Cultura," Supl. of *Novedades,* 586 (Jun. 5, 1960), p. 5.

———. "Carlos Pellicer; Voz viva de Mexico," Mexico: Universidad Nacional Autónoma de México, 1960, (record).

———. Review of *Material Poético,* "La Cultura en México," Supl. of *Siempre,* 16 (Jun. 6, 1962), p. III.

Aub, Max, ed. *Poesía Mexicana, 1950-1960.* Mexico: Aguilar, 1960.

Azuela, Salvador. "El ejemplo de Medellín Ostos," *El Universal* (Jul. 5, 1958).

Becerra, José Carlos. "La otra mirada," "El Gallo Ilustrado," Supl. of *El Día,* 333 (Mexico, Nov. 10, 1968), p. 3.

Blanco, Félix. *Poetas mexicanos.* Mexico: Editorial Diana, 1967.

Caillet-Bois, Julio. *Antología de la poesía hispanoamericana.* Madrid: Aguilar, 1965.

Calleros, Mario. "Las mesas de plomo. Carlos Pellicer," *Ovaciones,* Supl. 94 (Mexico, Oct. 13, 1963), p. 2.

Cantón Zetina, Carlos. "De arqueología, pintura y política habló Carlos Pellicer, quien dijo ser apolítico," *Excelsior* (Mexico, Mar. 13, 1966), p. 5-A.

Cantón, Wilberto. "Obligación del intelectual es la crítica al gobierno," *Novedades* (Mexico, Mar. 22, 1969), pp. 1, 7.

Carballo, Emmanual. "El libro de la semana," *Práctica de vuelo,* "México en la Cultura," Supl. of *Novedades,* 391 (Sept. 16, 1956), p. 2.

──────. "Carlos Pellicer o la poesía por la exageración," *Nivel,* 37 (Jan. 25, 1962), pp. 6, 7.

──────. "Conversación con Carlos Pellicer," "La Cultura en México," Supl. of *Siempre,* 16 (June 6, 1962), pp. III-VII.

──────. *19 (Diez y nueve) protagonistas de la literatura mexicana del siglo XX.* Mexico: Empresas Editoriales, 1965.

──────. "Cincuenta años de quehacer poético," "El Gallo Ilustrado," Supl. of *El Día,* 333 (Mexico, Nov. 10, 1968), p. 2.

Cardona Peña, Alfredo. "Carlos Pellicer," *Diario del Sureste* (Mérida, Yuc., June 6, 1949).

──────. "Carlos Pellicer," *Semblanzas mexicanas.* Mexico: Ediciones de Andrea, 1955, pp. 127-130.

──────. *"Material poético* de Carlos Pellicer," *El libro y el pueblo,* 44 (Mexico, Sept. 1968), pp. 24-28.

──────. "Cincuenta años de quehacer poético," "El Gallo Ilustrado," Supl. of *El Día,* 333 (Mexico, Nov. 10, 1968), p. 2.

Carrión, Benjamín. "Carlos Pellicer," *Revista de Indias,* 2 (Bogotá, 1939), pp. 212-222.

──────. *San Miguel de Unamuno.* Quito: Edit. Casa de la Cultura Ecuatoriana, 1954.

Castro, Rosa. "Y ahora hablemos de la poesía mexicana," *Hoy* (Mexico, Dec. 30, 1950).

Castro Leal, Antonio. *La poesía mexicana moderna.* Mexico: Fondo de Cultura Económica, 1953.

Cervera, Juan. "Ante un verso de Pellicer," *El Nacional* (Mexico, Dec. 1968), pp. 15-18.

Chumacero, Alí. "Un poeta juzga a otro poeta," "La Cultura en México," Supl. of *Siempre,* 16 (Jun. 6, 1962).

──────. "Con palabras y fuego," *La Gaceta del FCE* (Jan. 1963), p. 7.

──────. "Balance 1962: la poesía," "La Cultura en México," Supl. of *Siempre,* 46 (Jan. 2, 1963), p. IV.

Cohen, J. M. "The Eagel and the Serpent," *The Southern Review,* I:2, (Spring 1965), pp. 361-374.

Colín, Eduardo. *Rasgos.* Mexico: Imp. Manuel León Sánchez, 1934.

Comité de Acción Cultural. *Lista de libros representativos de América.* 2nd ed. Washington: Pan American Union, 1963.

146 REALITY AND EXPRESSION IN THE POETRY OF PELLICER

Cortázar, Manuel. "Rechazados del paraíso," *Siempre,* 820 (Mar. 12, 1969), p. 5.

Cuesta, Jorge. *Antología de la poesía mexicana moderna.* Mexico: Contemporáneos, 1928.

Cuevas, Rafael. *Panorámicas de las letras,* II, Mexico: Ediciones de la revista *Bellas Artes,* 1956.

Dauster, Frank. *Breve historia de la poesía mexicana.* Mexico: Ediciones de Andrea, 1956.

————. *Ensayos sobre la poesía mexicana.* Mexico: Ediciones de Andrea, 1963.

Díaz Ruanova, O. "Carlos Pellicer; el poeta," *Así* (Mexico, Dec. 30, 1940).

Espejo, Beatriz. "El poeta de la luz y del color," *El Rehilete,* 9 (Nov. 9, 1963), pp. 6-9.

Espinosa Altamirano, Horacio. "Tempestad para un poema de Carlos Pellicer," *Nivel,* 37 (Jan. 25, 1962), p. 9.

————. "La experiencia del viaje en Carlos Pellicer," *Boletín Bibliográfico de la Secretaría de Hacienda y Crédito Público,* IX: 274 (July 1, 1963), pp. 16-17.

Fernández, Eladio R. "Carlos Pellicer conserva hermosa tradición mexicana," *El Sol* (Mexico, Jan. 2, 1966), p. 5.

Fernández, Guillermo. "Unas palabras," "El Gallo Ilustrado," Supl. of *El Día,* 333 (Mexico, Nov. 10, 1968), p. 4.

Fitts, Dudley. *An Anthology of Contemporary Latin American Poetry.* 2nd ed., Norfolk, Connecticut: New Directions, 1947.

Florit, Eugenio. "'Ara Virginum' de Carlos Pellicer," *Revista Hispánica Moderna,* I:2 (New York, Jan.-April 1945), pp. 64-65.

Forster, Merlin H. *Los Contemporáneos, 1920-1932: perfil de un experimento vanguardista mexicano.* Mexico: Ediciones de Andrea, 1964.

————. "El Concepto de la creación poética en la obra de Carlos Pellicer," *Comunidad* IV:21 (Mexico, Oct. 1969), pp. 683-688.

Gálvez, Ramón. "Pausas literarias; *Hora de junio* de Carlos Pellicer," *Novedades,* Sunday Supl. (Mexico, Jun. 20, 1948), p. 2.

Gallo, Ugo y Guiseppi Bellini. *Storia della letteratura ispano-americana,* 2nd ed., Milan: Nuova Accademia Editrice, 1958.

Gamboa, Rubén Antonio. "El americanismo en la poesía de Carlos Pellicer," Master's Thesis. New Orleans, Tulane University, 1963.

————. "La poesía de Carlos Pellicer; búsqueda de la consubstancialidad," Ph.D. Dissertation, New Orleans, Tulane University.

Garibay, Ricardo. "Imágenes de Carlos Pellicer," "La Cultura en México," Supl. of *Siempre,* 38 (Nov. 7, 1962), p. XIII.

Gicovate, Bernard. "Carlos Pellicer; Material poético," *Handbook of Latin American Studies,* 26 (Gainesville, Fla., 1964), p. 176.

————. "Carlos Pellicer: Con palabras y fuego," *Handbook of Latin American Studies,* 28 (Gainesville, Fla., 1966), p. 281.

Gironella, Cecilia. "Perfiles; Carlos Pellicer clava mariposas, versos, y globos de navidad," *Hoy* (Mexico, Nov. 21, 1953).

Godoy, Emma. "La naturaleza, el hombre y Dios en la poesía de Carlos Pellicer," *El libro y el pueblo,* IV:3 (July 3, 1963), pp. 7-11, 31.

————. *Sombras de Magia.* Mexico: Fondo de Cultura Económica, 1968.

González de Mendoza, J. M. "*Hora y veinte* con Carlos Pellicer," *Repertorio Americano,* XX, pp. 88-95.

González Ramírez, Manuel y Rebeca Torres Ortega. *Poetas de México: Antología de la poesía contemporánea mexicana.* Mexico: Editorial America, 1945.

González Salas, Carlos. "La poesía mexicana actual," *Cuadernos Hispanoamericanos,* 104 (Madrid, August 1958), pp. 222-231.

——, ed. *Antología mexicana de poesía religiosa; Siglo veinte.* Mexico: Editorial Jus, 1960.

Gorostiza, José. "Cincuenta años de quehacer poético," "El Gallo Ilustrado," Supl. of *El Día,* 333 (Mexico, Nov. 10, 1968), p. 1.

Gringoire, Pedro. "Libros de nuestro tiempo Con palabras y fuego," *Excelsior* (Mexico, Jan. 10, 1963), p. 7-A.

Grucci, J. L. ed. *Three Spanish American Poets: Pellicer, Neruda, Andrade.* Alburquerque: Sage Books, 1942.

Henestrosa, Andrés. "La biblioteca de Carlos Pellicer," *El Nacional* (Mexico, July 12, 1968), p. 6.

Jarnes, Benjamín. "*Camino* y lección," *Ariel disperso.* Mexico: Stylo, 1946.

Karsen, Sonja. "Con palabras y fuego," *Books Abroad,* XXXVIII:2 (Spring 1964), pp. 176-177.

Labastida, Jaime. "Los sentidos solares de Carlos Pellicer, *Vida Nicolaita,* 10 (March 1965), pp. 8-9, 10.

Lambert, Jean-Clarence. *Les Poésies mexicaines.* Paris: Editions Seghers, 1961.

Latino, Simón. *Los cien mejores poemas latinoamericanos.* Buenos Aires: Editorial Nuestra América, 1963.

Leal, Luis. *Panorama de la literatura mexicana actual.* Washington: Pan American Union, 1968.

Leiva, Raúl. "La poesía de Carlos Pellicer," *Estaciones,* II:8 (Mexico, Winter 1957), pp. 378-395.

——. *Imagen de la poesía mexicana contemporánea.* Mexico: Imprenta Universitaria, 1959.

——. "Bibliografía por Carlos Pellicer," *Nivel,* 39 (March 25, 1962), pp. 2-3.

Lerín, Manuel. "Carlos Pellicer y el contorno de la poesía," *América,* 26 (Mexico, April 1944), pp. 21-31.

——. "Poesía reciente de Pellicer," *El Nacional* (Mexico, Dec. 26, 1948), pp. 5, 8.

Lloyd, Mallan. "Five Mexican Poets," *Poetry,* LXI:6 (Chicago, Mar. 1943), pp. 680-684.

Loera y Chávez, Agustín. "La joven literatura mexicana; Carlos Pellicer," *México Moderno,* I:5 (Mexico, Dec. 5, 1920), pp. 303-311.

Lugo, José María. "Esquemas para una religión del paisaje," *Armas y Letras,* VIII, 3 (Sept. 3, 1965), pp. 63-80.

Luquín, Eduardo. "Panorama de las letras mexicanas contemporáneas," *El Nacional,* Sunday Supl. (Mexico, Nov. 13, 1955), pp. 8, 9.

Magaña, Esquivel A. "Correo literario," *Diario del Sureste* (Mérida, Yuc., July 23, 1937).

Magdaleno, Mauricio. "Mediodía lírico de Pellicer," *El Universal* (Mexico, Nov. 30, 1948).

——. "Después del fin," *Todo* (Mexico, Nov. 24, 1955).

Maples Arce, Manuel. *Antología de la poesía mexicana moderna.* Rome: Poligráfica Tiberina, 1940.

Martínez, José Luis. *Literatura mexicana, siglo XX.* Mexico: Robredo, 1949.

——. "La literatura mexicana actual, 1954-1959," *Universidad de México,* XIV:4 (Mexico, Dec. 1959), pp. 11-17.

——. "Las letras Patrias," *México y la Cultura.* Mexico: Secretaría de Educación Pública, 1961.

Martínez Peñaloza, Porfirio. *Algunos epígonos del modernismo y otras notas.* Mexico: Ed. Camelina, 1966.

——. "Los primeros poemas de Carlos Pellicer," *Nivel* 70 (Mexico, Oct. 25, 1968), pp. 4, 8, 9.

Mediz Bolio, A. "La verdad en su lugar," *Repertorio Americano,* XX (San José, C.R., 1930), p. 285.

Mejía Sánchez, Ernesto. "Pellicer revisitado," *Novedades* (Mexico, Dec. 13, 1968), p. 5.

——. "Pellicer y Ahumada," *Novedades* (Mexico, Jan. 24, 1969), p. 5.

——. "El año Pellicer," *Novedades* (Mexico, Mar. 24, 1969), p. 5.

Mendoza, María Luisa. "*Una hora de junio* con Carlos Pellicer," "El Gallo Ilustrado," Supl. of *El Día,* 1 (Mexico, July 1, 1962), p. 1.

——. "Yo no sé nada de Pellicer," "El Gallo Ilustrado," Supl. of *El Día,* 333 (Mexico, Nov. 10, 1968), p. 4.

Mendoza, Miguel Angel. "Existe una crisis en la poesía mexicana," *Novedades* (Mexico, July 3, 17, 24, and Aug. 14, 1949).

Mirador. "Belvedere; Carlos Pellicer," *Novedades* (Mexico, April 8, 1967), p. 4.

Mistral, Gabriela. "Un poeta nuevo de América; Carlos Pellicer Cámara," *Repertorio Americano,* XIV: 34 (San José, C. R., 1927), p. 373.

Mojarro, Tomás. "Cincuenta años de quehacer poético," "El Gallo Ilustrado," Supl. of *El Día,* 333 (Mexico, Nov. 10, 1968), p. 2.

Monguío, Luis. "Poetas post-modernistas mexicanos," *Revista Hispánica Moderna,* XII: 3-4 (July-Oct. 1946), pp. 239-266.

Monsivais, Carlos. "Homenaje a tres poetas: Pellicer, Chumacero, Cernuda," "La Cultura en México," Supl. of *Siempre,* 150 (Mexico, Dec. 30, 1964), pp. I-III.

——. *La poesía mexicana del siglo XX.* Mexico: Empresas Editoriales, 1966, pp. 31-36, 361.

——. "Carlos Pellicer; el agua de los cántaros sabe a pájaro," "La Cultura en México," Supl. of *Siempre,* 377 (Mexico, May 7, 1969), p. XVI.

Montezuma de Carvalho, Joaquim de. *Panorama das literaturas das Américas; de 1900 a actualidade.* Vol. IV. Angola: Edicao do Municipio de Nova Lisboa, 1963.

Mora, Ángel. "Plano literario de México," *Así* (Mexico, June 16, 1945).

Moreno Villa, José. *Doce manos mexicanas.* Mexico: Ed. Loera y Chávez, 1941.

Mullen, E. J. "The Critics and Carlos Pellicer," *USF Language Quarterly,* XI (Fall-winter, 1972), pp. 39-40.

Novaro, Octavio. "Paseo por Villahermosa con Carlos Pellicer," "México en la Cultura," Supl. of *Novedades,* Aug. 20, 1972, p. 3.

Novo, Salvador. *La vida en México en el período presidencial de Miguel Alemán.* México: Empresas Editoriales, 1967.

——. "Cincuenta años de quehacer poético," "El Gallo Ilustrado," Supl. of *El Día,* 333 (Mexico, Nov. 10, 1968), p. 1.

Ocampo de Gómez, Aurora M. and Ernesto Prado Velázquez. *Diccionario de escritores mexicanos*. Mexico: Universidad Nacional Autónoma de México, 1967.

Onís, Federico de. *Antología de la poesía española e hispanoamericana, 1882-1932*. Madrid: Casa Editorial Hernando, 1934.

Ortiz de Montellano, Bernardo. "Un camino de poesía," *Contemporáneos*, V, 16 (Mexico, Sept. 1929), pp. 150-152.

Pacheco, José Emilio. "El que ama la vida y las palabras," "La Cultura en México," Supl. of *Siempre*, 16 (June 16, 1962), p. VI.

Pacheco, León. "Mexicanos en París," "México en la cultura," Supl. of *Novedades*, 726 (Mexico, Feb. 17, 1963), p. 9.

Pam. "El arte debe reflejar la vida de un país; Pellicer," *Excelsior* (Mexico, June 20, 1964).

Pardo García, Germán. "A Carlos Pellicer; ofreciéndole el libro *Hay piedras como lágrimas*," Nivel, 37 (Mexico, Jan. 27, 1962), p. 6.

Pavón, Francisco. "Gravitación de lo indígena en la poesía de Carlos Pellicer," Ph. D. Dissertation, Rutgers University, 1969.

Paz, Octavio. "La poesía de Carlos Pellicer," *Revista Mexicana de Literatura*, 5 (Mexico, May-June 1956), pp. 486-493.

————. *Las peras del olmo*. Mexico: Imprenta Universitaria, 1957.

————, ed. *Poesía en movimiento, México 1915-1966*. Mexico: Siglo XXI, 1966.

Peñalosa, Javier. "Nombres, títulos y hechos," "México en la Cultura," Supl. of *Novedades*, 780 (March 1, 1964), p. 5.

Perera Mena, Alfredo. *Breve discourso por Carlos Pellicer*. Mexico: Ed. Prisma, 1964.

Pereyra, Gabriel. "La Anahuacali de Diego Rivera y una conversación con Carlos Pellicer," *El Día* (Mexico, Nov. 16, 1964).

————. "Colección Carlos Pellicer donada por el poeta al pueblo de Tepotztlán," *El Día* (June 16, 1965), p. 9.

Pérez, Gutiérrez, Leticia. "El agua en la obra poética de Carlos Pellicer," *Humanitas* (Universidad de Nuevo León, 1971), pp. 133-151.

Ponce de Hurtado, Teresa. *El ruiseñor lleno de muerte*. Mexico: Editorial Meridiano, 1970.

Poniatowska, Elena. "Nadie es 'Tan Jardín'; Carlos Pellicer," "El Gallo Ilustrado," Supl. of *El Día* 333 (Mexico, Nov. 10, 1964), p. 9.

————. *Palabras cruzadas*. Mexico: Biblioteca Era, 1961.

Prats, Alardo. "A los 50 años de hacer poesía ...," *Novedades* (Mexico, Nov. 17, 1968), p. 6.

Puga, Mario. "Carlos Pellicer," *Universidad de México*, X:6 (Feb. 1956), pp. 16-19.

R. V. B. "Carlos Pellicer Cámera: Poeta de América," *El Universal*, April 16, 1972, pp. 4, 5.

Rico Galán, Victor. "El mundo literario," *Impacto*, 39 (Mexico, April 22, 1950), p. 111.

Roggiano, Alfredo A. "*Material poético*," *Revista Iberoamericana*, XXVIII: 54 (July-Dec. 1962), pp. 407-412.

————. *En este aire de América*. Mexico: Ed. Cultura, 1966.

————. "*Material poético*," México en la Cultura, Supl. of *Novedades*, 914 (Sept. 25, 1966), p. 3.

Rojas Garcidueñas, José. "Estridentismo y contemporáneos," *Universidad de México*, VI, 72 (December 1952).

Romero, Manuel Antonio. "Carlos Pellicer, huésped de la Tierra," *América,* 55 (Mexico, Feb. 29, 1948), pp. 48-66.

Rosaldo, Renato. "The Legacy of Literature and Art," in *Six Faces of Mexico.* Tucson: University of Arizona Press, 1966, p. 299.

Ruís, Luis. "El *Material poético* de Carlos Pellicer," *Cuadernos Americanos,* XXI, CXXIV: 5 (Sept.-Oct. 1962), pp. 239-270.

Ruíz Medrano, José. *Lira.* Mexico: Editorial Jus., 1963.

Sainz, Gustavo. "Carlos Pellicer," *Sur,* 272 (Buenos Aires, Sept.-Oct. 1961), p. 37.

Santamaría, Francisco J. *La poesía tabasqueña, Antología.* Mérida, Yucatan: Editorial Yucatanense, 1950.

Schlak, Carolyn Brandt. "The Poetry of Carlos Pellicer," Ph. D. Dissertation, Denver: University of Colorado, 1957.

Segerskog, Birgitta. "Graves ranks Pellicer, Paz among best of Mexican poets," *The News* (Mexico, Oct. 13, 1968), p. 17.

Selva, Mauricio de la. "Astericos," *Excelsior* (May 16, 1965), p. 4-A.

Sevilla, Juan de. "Carlos Pellicer," *El Nacional,* 35 (Mexico, Nov. 24, 1968), p. 1.

Sierra Partida, Alfonso. "La biblioteca de Carlos Pellicer," *El Nacional* (July 12, 1968).

Suárez, Luis. "Impresiones de un viaje por Hispanoamérica," "México en la Cultura," Supl. of *Novedades,* 546 (August 30, 1959), p. 1, 4.

Suárez, Martín. "Dios y Pellicer," "El Gallo Ilustrado," Supl. of *El Día,* 1 (Mexico, July 1, 1962), p. 2.

Tiquet, José. "Carlos Pellicer," *Lectura,* XCVI: 2 (Mexico, Nov. 15, 1953), pp. 44-52.

Torres Bodet, Jaime. *Contemporáneos; Notas de crítica.* Mexico: Herrero, 1928.

———. *Tiempo de arena.* México: Fondo de Cultura Económica, 1955.

———. *Trebol de cuatro hojas.* Mexico: University Veracruzana, 1960.

Torres-Rioseco, Arturo and Ralph E. Warner. *Bibliografía de la poesía mexicana.* Cambridge: Harvard University Press, 1934.

Usigli, Rodolfo. "Carlos Pellicer," *Letras de México,* 6 (Mexico, April 16, 1937), pp. 1-2.

Vela, Arqueles. "Inmemorial a Carlos Pellicer," "México en la Cultura," Supl. of *Novedades,* 874 (Dec. 19, 1965), p. 3.

———. *Fundamentos de la literatura mexicana.* 2nd ed. Mexico: Ed. Patria, 1966, pp. 124-125.

———. *Poemontaje.* Mexico: Ediciones de Andrea, 1968.

Venegas, Roberto. "Poetas mexicanos: Carlos Pellicer," *Excelsior* (July 26, 1964), pp. 3A, 7A.

Villaurrutia, Xavier. "Cartas a Olivier," *Ulises,* I, 2 (June 1927).

———. "La poesía de los jóvenes de México." (Lecture read in the Libreria Cervantes), Mexico, 1924.

Xirau, Ramón. "Los hechos y la cultura," *Nivel* (Mexico, Jan. 26, 1962), p. 12.

———. *Tres poetas de la soledad.* Mexico: Robredo, 1955, p. 9.

Zaid, Gabriel. "Homenaje a la alegría," "La Cultura en México," Supl. of *Siempre* 248 (Nov. 16, 1966), p. XX.

Zendejas, Francisco. "Multilibros," *Excelsior* (Mexico, Jan. 17, 1962), p. 17.